Fresh Views
on Resilient Living

Fresh Views
on Resilient Living

Sharon Pam Eakes, MA, BCC

FRESH VIEWS ON RESILIENT LIVING
Copyright © 2015 by Sharon Pam Eakes

All rights reserved. No part of this publication may be reproduced, distributed, or transmitted in any form or by any means, including photocopying, recording, or other electronic or mechanical methods, without the prior written permission of the author, except in the case of brief quotations embodied in critical reviews and certain other noncommercial uses permitted by copyright law. For permission requests, write to the author, at the address below.

This book is designed to provide information and motivation to our readers. It is sold with the understanding that the publisher is not engaged to render any type of psychological, legal, or any other kind of professional advice. The content of each article is the sole expression and opinion of its author, and not necessarily that of the publisher. No warranties or guarantees are expressed or implied by the publisher's choice to include any of the content in this volume. Neither the publisher nor the author shall be liable for any physical, psychological, emotional, financial, or commercial damages, including, but not limited to, special, incidental, consequential or other damages. Our views and rights are the same: You are responsible for your own choices, actions, and results.

To contact the author, Sharon Pam Eakes, visit:
  Website ....: www.hopellc.com
  Email ....: sharon@hopellc.com
  LinkedIn ....: www.linkedin.com/pub/sharon-eakes/0/941/858

Printed in the United States of America

To contact the publisher, inCredible Messages Press, visit www.inCredibleMessages.com

ISBN 978-0-9908265-2-1 paperback
ISBN 978-0-9908265-3-8 eBook

SELF-HELP / Personal Growth / Happiness

Book coach .... : Bonnie Budzowski
Cover design .... : Barbara Curry
Zendoodles .... : Aleta Akhtar
Author photograph .... : Annie Gensheimer

Praise for Fresh Views

I like "Fresh Views" because they are short and easy to read, yet thought provoking and always helpful. They inevitably speak to an important and still-growing part of my life. I also love Sharon's style!

Paul Overby
Business Executive

I enjoy reading "Fresh Views" and always take away some little nugget of information. An essay may just plant a seed in my brain that I later recognize as it's blooming into a useful tool for living life wisely. I love reading of your own personal experiences and find myself both relating to them and being inspired by them. Sometimes the biggest takeaway is just one word that resonates with me and I will find myself pondering it over and over.

Annie Gensheimer
Photographer

I always love to see "Fresh Views" show up, and particularly like that they tend to come right in the middle of the work day. They are sort of like a moment of fresh air/natural light in the middle of a fluorescent-lit afternoon. I usually end up laughing and feeling more grounded, and then get back to work. I suspect that other people do the same.

Kathleen McTigue, MD

I read "Fresh Views" because I like stories. They help me to look at the world through someone else's eyes a little differently. I tell them to others and that helps me to connect. Small interactions and little systems, I believe, are the glue that hold the big systems together. The stories help me to imagine, to hope, and to do.

Rathindra Roy
Development Facilitator/Consultant

I read "Fresh Views" usually when I don't really have time to be reading emails. However, whenever I read them usually I can apply some part of what you have to say to my business or my family.

Patty Hinkle
Business Owner

What I really like about "Fresh Views" is that they offer real inspirational gems—they stay with me, usually for at least two weeks or so and they make me look at things anew. Thank you for sharing this brilliant gift.

Dr. Astrid Kersten
Professor of Management

I receive your "Fresh Views" and want to thank you for sharing your thoughts. They offer "real help" by providing gentle reminders to refocus on what is truly important. That's no small feat, especially on hectic days. Thanks again!

Jody Adams, M.A., CPO

I always find your "Fresh Views" inspiring and they usually motivate me into dealing with everyday events in a new way. For instance, this idea you have about planting seeds is giving me permission to think that I really want to learn to play classical piano. Since I inherited my mother's piano years ago, it seems just to decorate our guesthouse. Every time I go in there, I want to sit down and play it like my mother used to.

Joan Peterson
Poet

Each month I look forward to the day when I'll have a short break with "Fresh Views" from Sharon Eakes. They are always thought provoking, always relevant, and often provide exactly the inspiration I need to untangle whatever knot I'm working on.

Sharon Lippincott
Author, Adventures of a Chilehead

I look forward to "Fresh Views" popping up on my computer screen. I am frequently surprised with the timeliness of your writings. So often, what you have written can readily be associated to what is going on in my life just then. The serendipity quality is very appealing.

Second, I love your examples after you define clearly what you are going to write about. All of your examples are easy to relate to, but frequently they are ones that I would not have related to the topic you are writing about. In that sense, I have been able to learn a lot.

Third, so many of your articles have been framed within the context of systems thinking. You have written really well on that whole concept. I have learned a lot from what you have written and have gone on to ask myself, particularly with respect to world issues, how does the systems approach affect the outcome of a given situation? I have also thought of this in terms of interpersonal relationships.

I am so delighted that you are putting together a collection of your gems. I think I have made that wish to you often in these past years and it is wonderful that the wish will be coming true!

Marnie Haines

I read "Fresh Views" every month because there is always at least one element that I can relate to directly. On a number of occasions, the subject has turned out to be like a mini-counseling session for me, to handle a real-time challenging situation with my wife, our kids, or work. You've set up a good conditioning routine, because it's a pleasure to open the message, see the friendly title, read the quote, and then dig into the main course. Please sign me up to buy one of the first copies of the book!

Gerry Katilius
Google Manager

I enjoy your "Fresh Views" for the mental stimulation they provide, the new perspectives they bring, and the coaching tips you provide. I look forward to receiving them each month.

Dr. Ian Metcalfe
Dialogic Facilitator/Consultant

Dedication

To my precious children, stepchildren, grandchildren, and great-grandchildren. May you be resilient!

CONTENTS

FOREWORD 1

INTRODUCTION: FRESH VIEWS ON RESILIENT LIVING 5

CHAPTER 1 TAP THE INCREDIBLE POWER OF THE MIND 13
    1-1 Thinking 19
    1-2 Thinking Styles 22
    1-3 What We Focus on Grows 24
    1-4 Habits 26
    1-5 Metaphors 29
    1-6 Wabi-Sabi 31
    1-7 Novelty 33
    1-8 Learn and Forget 36
    1-9 Forgetting 39
    1-10 Questions 42
    1-11 Intention vs. Expectation 44
    1-12 Developing Ideas 48
    1-13 Make Mistakes 50
    1-14 Go to the Balcony 53
    1-15 Decision Making 55
    1-16 Invent a Better Story 58
    1-17 Inspiration 61

CHAPTER 2 CREATE RELATIONSHIPS THAT WORK 65
    2-1 Relationships 69
    2-2 Interdependence 72
    2-3 Listening 75
    2-4 Walk a Mile 78
    2-5 From Blame to Accountability 81
    2-6 Differences and Curiosity 84
    2-7 Conflict 86

2-8 Solving Circles 89
2-9 What Are You Carrying? 91
2-10 No Sniveling! 94
2-11 Do What You Say You'll Do 96
2-12 Appreciate 99
2-13 Learning from a Penguin Trainer 102
2-14 Penguin Training II 104
2-15 Choose in Every Moment 107
2-16 Shifts of Heart 111
2-17 Encouragement 114
2-18 Generosity 116
2-19 Kindness 118

CHAPTER 3 BE UPBEAT 121
3-1 Breathe 125
3-2 Be Happy 127
3-3 Don't Seek Balance 130
3-4 What's Right? 132
3-5 Helping Things Go Right 135
3-6 Stopping and Starting 138
3-7 Emotions 141
3-8 Silence 144
3-9 Expect Surprises 146
3-10 Effortlessness 149
3-11 Be Early 152
3-12 Patience 155
3-13 Fun 158
3-14 Take a Break 161
3-15 Gratitude 165
3-16 Comfort Zones 169
3-17 Aging Well 173

Chapter 4 Stay Energized 175
- 4-1 Goals that Inspire 179
- 4-2 Noticing 182
- 4-3 Enough 185
- 4-4 Ten Delicious Daily Habits.................................... 188
- 4-5 Hurrying... 191
- 4-6 Navigating Your Experience................................. 194
- 4-7 Choices.. 197
- 4-8 Humor 199
- 4-9 Attention Not Energy.. 202
- 4-10 Play 205
- 4-11 10-10-10 Rule 209
- 4-12 Sleep... 212
- 4-13 Decay is Optional... 215
- 4-14 Celebrate!.. 218

Chapter 5 See Connections Everywhere 221
- 5-1 Maintaining Systems.. 227
- 5-2 Managing System Delays 230
- 5-3 Living with Terrorism... 233
- 5-4 Do Something Different....................................... 236
- 5-5 Seasons.. 239
- 5-6 Small Systems... 242
- 5-7 Transitions and Systems 245
- 5-8 Make Room.. 247
- 5-9 If You're Stuck, Clean a Closet 250
- 5-10 Say No to Say Yes 252
- 5-11 Holding On and Letting Go 255
- 5-12 Limits to Growth... 258
- 5-13 Perfecting Environments................................... 261
- 5-14 Deepening 264

CHAPTER 6 GIVING BACK 267
    6-1 Purpose 271
    6-2 Gifts from the Heart 275
    6-3 Real Help 278
    6-4 Initiative 282
    6-5 Jen Ratio 284
    6-6 Life—A Work of Art...287
    6-7 Contribution 289

CONCLUSION: RESILIENT LIVING 293

ACKNOWLEDGEMENTS.. 299

ABOUT THE AUTHOR 303

Foreword

During the early months of 2000, I was seeking a new columnist who would write about wellness for the readers of our free community newspaper, the *Green Tree Times*. Jack Walsh, our ad salesperson, suggested several professionals who were advertisers, but I kept saying, "No, no, I don't think so."

Jack finally asked me somewhat impatiently, "Well, what do you want?"

I said, "I want a writer I can trust to help our readers embrace their lives with acceptance of what is and to become open to making changes to improve their lives. I want someone who is wise, authentic, caring, and down-to-earth."

Jack said, "I know exactly the right person—Sharon Eakes."

Throughout these 15 years through her *Musings* column, Sharon has written with humor and insight about many of her own life lessons. She is brilliant, compassionate, and a persuasive writer and life coach who gently guides readers along new pathways of thinking. She gives our readers the hope and tools for change as well as suggestions on how to stay lively and fully engaged in their own lives.

We are all tremendously grateful to have Sharon in our lives.

Peg Stewart, publisher
Green Tree Times

Introduction:

Fresh Views on Resilient Living

Fresh Views on Resilient Living

The Way is long—Let us go together.
The Way is difficult—Let us help each other.
The Way is joyful—Let us share it.
The Way is ours alone—Let us go in love.
The Way grows before us—Let us begin.
– Zen Invocation

IN A WELL-KNOWN PARABLE, four blind men are arguing about the essential nature of an elephant. The man in front says the elephant is "like a huge, rough hose." The man on the side describes the elephant as "like a tree trunk." The man in the back says the elephant is "rope-like." And the man two feet behind says the elephant is "soft, mushy and close to the ground." Each person is, of course, absolutely right. There are many ways to view any subject, depending on your perspective.

This book is about perspectives. In 2000, I began writing short essays in a monthly e-newsletter called *Fresh Views*. Each essay was also published each month in the *Green Tree Times* as *Musings*. In these essays, I invite readers to view an everyday subject from new perspectives. My goal is always to provoke, inspire, and nudge readers to think, stretch, smile, and grow.

Most months *Fresh Views* has been followed by a telegathering where readers join me to explore the subject more deeply. These cyber meetings are always a treat, as more perspectives are added to the mix and we are all enriched in the process.

For years, people have encouraged me to gather these short essays into a book. When I finally considered that seriously, I asked myself: What do the essays all add up to? What is it that I have to contribute? The best answer I've found is that the perspectives I embrace all add up to a happy, resilient life. Which is exactly what I have. I feel like the luckiest woman in the world! At 70+, I could be called an old woman, yet I feel young. Life has not spared me heartache or difficulties. Yet I have an interesting, adventuresome, uplifting, fun life. (For more about me, see About the Author at the end of the book.)

Since I've been around for many decades, I have a rich pool of experience and sources of influence from which to draw fresh perspectives. Along the way, I've also been fortunate to play many interesting roles: college teacher, therapist, clinical director of a drug and alcohol treatment program, personal and executive coach, workshop facilitator, teacher, and author. With my husband, Hal, I wrote *Liberating Greatness, a Whole Brain Guide to an Extraordinary Life*, in 2006. Hal was an expert on the brain, and I learned a great deal from both what he knew and how he lived his knowledge.

My perspectives have been strongly influenced by the work of Peter Senge. In 1990, Senge wrote *The Fifth Discipline* in which he identified the five disciplines of a learning organization. Intended as a college text, the book sold over a million copies, was translated into 120 languages, and brought a new way of thinking to many areas of life: business, education, and healthcare to name a few. Three of the five disciplines are often the focus of my work: Mental Models, Personal Mastery, and Systems Thinking. The importance of how we think and the ways in which things and people are intricately interconnected fascinate and delight me.

In 2001, a wonderful couple, Farid and Fara Samandari, attended one of the month-long seminars Hal and I facilitated. Through them we discovered and fell in love with the Bahá'í Faith. In 2002, Hal and I became members of the Bahá'í Faith, and it has been one of the best decisions I ever made. This modern, independent, global religion gives perspective, guidance, hope, and a sense of purpose beyond what we ever imagined. The goal set out in the Bahá'í sacred writings is one of unity, peace, and an ever-advancing civilization. I am committed to working toward those goals, and my writing is influenced by that commitment.

Some years ago, I discovered the Arbinger Institute, whose philosophy thrills me! It gives every spiritual tradition legs. I'm now co-facilitator of a master coaching course by phone that helps coaches around the world utilize this bounty.

Perhaps the richest source of wisdom has come from the important relationships in my life: being a wife, mother, grandmother, great-grandmother, coach, friend, and companion to a quirky cat.

As a coach and writer, I love helping people to identify and develop their natural gifts. I'm interested in tuning my own life so that it feels purposeful, uses my thinking and my energy in the best possible ways, and is also of service to others. I'm fascinated with the fact that I can be old and wise in so many ways and still find myself stuck, doing things that don't work well, being human.

I love learning from others, and translating complex theories and solutions from various disciplines into understandable language. I like ideas that are simple and elegant, tried and true, and that pierce to the heart of things.

This book is meant to be down-to-earth and practical, while tapping the wisdom of the wise from every discipline: business, philosophy, psychology, and theology. Pay particular attention to the quotes that begin each essay. They are integral to the meaning.

The essays are organized into six sections:

1. **TAP THE INCREDIBLE POWER OF THE MIND**
   Essays in this section are about combining our brains and hearts to use the full capacity of our minds.

2. **CREATE RELATIONSHIPS THAT WORK**
   The tricky and wonderful world of relationships is at the heart of both most of our joy and much of our tension. The essays in this section will guide us to reflect on our relationships and the perspectives we bring to them.

3. **BE UPBEAT**
   Life can be difficult. What would it mean to your quality of life if you could always come back to cheerful? The essays in this section consider just how you might do that.

4. **STAY ENERGIZED**
   We all need to find ways to sustain ourselves over the long haul. The essays in this section explore ways in which we have control over our own energy as well as ways in which we self-sabotage.

5. **SEE CONNECTIONS EVERYWHERE**
   Nothing exists in a vacuum—every little piece seems hooked to every other little piece in life. Essays in this section show how building an awareness of interconnectedness can change outcomes.

6. **GIVE BACK**
   Essays in this section explore the notion that each of us, as we realize our own true potential, is helping to realize the true potential of civilization.

Taken together, these pieces add up to resilience. Some synonyms for resilient are supple, tough, expansive, and quick to recover. This is the kind of life I want—for myself and for you.

Before you even start, I beg your forgiveness for one thing. Because I chose to organize the book by topic instead of chronology, you may find some odd leaps required. I often use my own experience to illustrate something, and because of that, and the fact that the pieces aren't in chronological order, you may find that my husband Hal has died in one piece and is riding his bike in the next. You will even find I refer to my late husband Gene in one essay, because I've had more than one husband. (See About the Author section for more details.) Thanks for being a flexible reader.

Each piece was written to stand alone, so feel free to read a little here and there, keep the book in the bathroom, use it as a source of conversation with your family—read it backwards, from the middle; it's not a straight through read. Or try what one reader described as her "favorite game." Read the quote. Make it the jumping off point for dinner conversation with your family or friends. Then read my perspective on it.

Embedded in this book is my deep belief that people are meant to be happy, to live useful and rewarding lives, to bounce back from inevitable difficulties, and that such lives are truly possible. Enjoy!

Chapter 1

Tap the Incredible Power of the Mind

Tap the Incredible Power of the Mind

The greatest revolution in our generation is the discovery that human beings, by changing the inner attitudes of their minds, can change the outer aspects of their lives.

— William James

I can't remember which I fell in love with first—the brain or my husband, Hal. During my time as Clinical Director at Gateway Rehabilitation Center, Hal delivered an amazing seminar over four days to the patients and staff. Called "Pathways to Greatness," the seminar was about the neural pathways in the brain. Hal's own remarkable story was the inspiration for the seminar.

Diagnosed "retarded" in elementary school, Hal studied day and night, eventually becoming an engineer and a patent attorney. As a young adult, Hal found that alcohol calmed the anxiety that he'd be found out as a fraud, because he was really "retarded." Hal became an alcoholic. When he sobered up, someone introduced him to the Herrmann Brain Dominance Instrument that measures thinking style preferences. When Hal saw his own results—that he was creative and liked people—he came to understand that he preferred to think differently from many others. He certainly thought differently from most engineers and lawyers. He began to study the brain as a hobby.

Originally, Hal put a seminar together for other recovering alcoholics. He wanted to help them move forward with their lives and thought an understanding of the brain's capabilities would help. Eventually Hal was invited to deliver that seminar to all of the people in the aerospace company where he was a patent attorney.

By the time Hal brought the seminar to Gateway, he had left the practice of law and was taking this hopeful program to groups of all kinds. I was hooked immediately—both on the brain and on Hal. We were married six months later. In 1996, I left Gateway and joined Hal's training and consulting company, Hope Unlimited, LLC. I trained as a coach and added coaching to the services offered. I joined Hal in the study of the brain as well.

When I think of how hard it is for the mind to understand itself, I laugh. We think we're so smart, yet we keep finding the brain is capable of things we never imagined. For example, for most of the 25 years I was involved in drug and alcohol treatment, it was widely accepted that the brain was the only organ in the body that didn't regenerate itself. So, we told patients, once you kill off a bunch of brain cells with alcohol or drugs, those are gone forever.

As soon as technology made it possible to watch the brain in real time, however, researchers discovered that our assumption was wrong. The brain makes new stem cells all the time and these cells run around trying to fix things, (which doesn't mean you should keep drinking or using drugs). Scientists have even discovered things we can do to help make new brain cells: exercise, learn something new, and meditate!

We know that if you imagine and visualize doing something repeatedly, the effect is almost the same as if you actually do it. You can practice in your mind. The early work in visualization compared how two groups performed in basketball, throwing free throws. The first group actually practiced, throwing the ball. The second group only imagined practicing—throwing perfect throws in their imaginations. In the end, guess what? The performance of the two groups was virtually identical.

We've learned that there are brain cells in the heart and the gut. We don't yet know how these combine with qualities like spirit to make the mind. But we know the mind has incredible capacity. We've learned that the power of intention is so strong, for example, a paraplegic can steer a boat with her mind.

We've come to understand that people think and learn differently, and that continuing to learn is possible until the day we die. In fact, one thing that keeps the mind young is learning new things.

So many people at the seminars Hal and I conducted asked, "Where is the book?" As a result, we made that seminar into a book, published in 2006 with the title, *Liberating Greatness, the Whole Brain Guide to an Extraordinary Life.* Ned Herrmann's work at General Electric had sparked our interest in the brain, but Hal and I soon found many other brain scientists to be of great interest. Bruce Lipton, Jeffrey Schwartz, and Sharon Begley were among our early favorites. Daniel Goleman and David Rock have influenced me as they've applied new understanding of the brain to coaching. Stephanie West Allen continues to delight me with her blog www.BrainsOnPurpose.com.

Over the years, I've written about the brain in a variety of ways, which you'll see in this section.

I figure we've only scratched the surface as far as the mind goes, but what we do know is awe inspiring! I invite you to explore the power of your mind as you read the essays in this section. Understanding the power of your own thinking can change your life!

1~1

THINKING

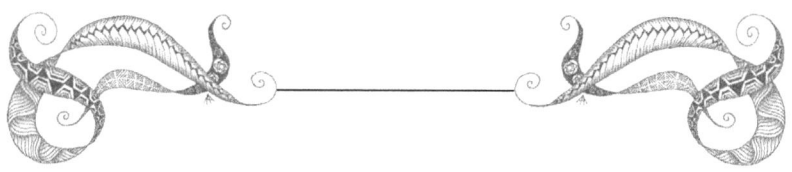

Few people think more than two or three times a year. I have made an international reputation for myself by thinking once a week.
— George Bernard Shaw

WHEN MY SON GORDON WAS EIGHT, I came upon him sitting on the couch one day doing absolutely nothing. He was not watching TV or playing a game or reading. I asked, somewhat accusingly, "What are you doing?" His answer was quick. "Thinking," he said. "Is that OK?" The event stuck in my mind. How unusual it is in our culture to just stop and think.

James Hackett, President and CEO of Steelcase, described his company's examination of a product launch failure. A key discovery was that the team put all its energy into execution before thinking the idea through. "When people told me that the one thing they could use more of was time, what they were really saying was that they needed more time to think." (*Harvard Business Review*, April 2007)

Though many people yearn for the time to think things through and to have deep, thinking conversations, it would be surprising to see "think time" scheduled on anybody's calendar. Yet, why not? One reason I think coaching is so popular is that it builds in time specifically to stop, think, reflect, and connect thoughts. *Aha* moments often come from slight shifts of thinking or seeing new connections between things.

Reflection

Thinking quietly by ourselves is called reflection. Stopping to reflect on our thoughts, actions, emotions, and plans can prevent a lot of grief. It can also be the source of learning from our experience as we move through life.

I once heard this prescription: any personal problem can be solved if you are willing to sit with it for four hours. Ask a very clear question, the guideline said, and then be still as your brain, conscious and unconscious, plays with possibilities. By the end of four hours, you were promised an answer. I did it only once—sitting at the ocean—and it was practically magic. After feeling absolutely lost, at about three hours, I suddenly had an aha, clarity, and a plan of action.

Collaboration

Thinking together is often called collaboration, and can be exhilarating. You know this if you have had deep, thoughtful conversations with one or more people about something that matters to you. The World Café is a way to encourage such conversations in groups. It often leads to breakthrough thinking. (See www.TheWorldCafe.org.)

If We Don't Think

If we forget to stop and think, either by ourselves or with others, one common result is that we hurry toward a destination, busily doing everything it takes to get there, without really considering whether this is where we want to go.

Coaching Tips and Questions

- How often do you think deeply about things that matter to you?
- When was the last time you stopped to think about whether the things on your to-do list will get you where you want to go?
- Who are your best thought partners?
- What would you love to spend some time thinking about deeply?
- What would it take to schedule some "think time" into your life either alone or with others?
- Winnie the Pooh asked, "Did you ever stop to think and forget to start again?" I recommend it!

1~2
Thinking Styles

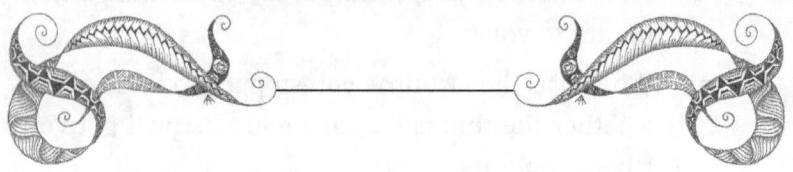

The different views offered by the members of a [group] are like the ingredients of a delicious stew.
— Hushmand Fathea'zam

People think differently. The differences show up in work styles, decision-making, communication, and problem solving. Some people are collaborators while others prefer to work alone. People are drawn to either the big picture or the details. Some like information delivered in succinct bullets, others like expressive stories. These differences can be a source of conflict or celebration. You choose.

I was once facilitating a workshop using the Herrmann Brain Dominance Instrument (HBDI), which assesses and explores thinking styles. At a break, an agitated participant approached and asked if he could be excused just long enough to call his wife in Kuala Lumpur. They had had a big fight the night before he left for the states, and he had decided she was crazy. With relief, he said, "She's not crazy, she's just right brained!"

Coaching Tips and Questions

- What is your thinking style? Are you Analytical? Organized? Emotional? Creative? Get to know your own thinking style preferences by taking the HBDI at http://hopellc.com/bdsi.html.

- Accept that people truly see the world through different lenses.

- Do not take it personally when someone has a perspective different from yours. They are not just trying to bug you.

- Think of a person you know who thinks very differently from you. How can you approach that person with curiosity instead of defensiveness?

- For the richest result when forming a team, seek diversity of thinkers.

- When you are stuck, ask for input from people who think very differently than you.

1-3

WHAT WE FOCUS ON GROWS

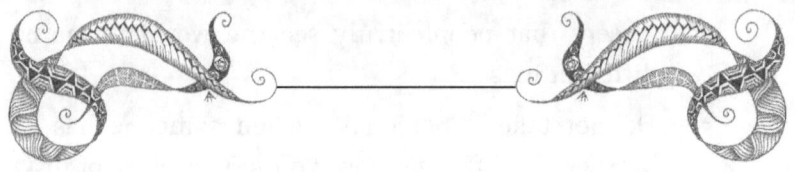

You see what you want to see.
– The Rockman in the musical *The Point*

While I was weeding my rambunctious country garden, I realized a funny thing. When I go after a particular kind of weed, that weed becomes all I see. I do not see other weeds or the flowers around them. I become so focused that I am like a one-woman cavalry going after crabgrass. Then I switch to another weed, and that is all I see. This experience brought home a couple of truths:

- We can only see one thing at a time. Literally. Our brains can shift quickly, but we can only focus on one thing at a time.
- What we focus on grows.
- These truths apply whether the focus is weeds, blame, gratitude, what's working, or what's not working in our lives.

Examples

- When we decide things are a certain way, we do not see evidence to the contrary.

- When we are consciously grateful for many little things in our lives, we find more things to be grateful for and generally feel happier.
- When we are blaming someone for something, we find more and more evidence to reinforce our blaming. The more we focus on the blaming, the more we become angry and upset.

Coaching Tips and Questions

- Make thoughtful choices about what you want to see.
- Focus on what you want to grow.
- Make a list of 10 things for which you are grateful.
- Choose three things you want to grow. How can you focus on these three things?

1-4
Habits

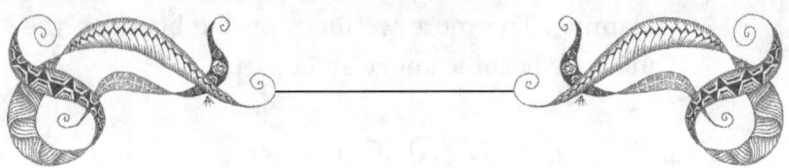

We are what we repeatedly do. Excellence, then, is not an act, but a habit.

– Aristotle

According to the dictionary, a habit is "an acquired behavior pattern regularly followed until it has become almost involuntary." Since we repeatedly think and do many of the same things every day, each of us has developed many habits, some comforting and supportive, others negative and destructive.

Examples

- The route we use to drive to work or the grocery store
- The way we treat people
- The food we eat
- The way we spend our free time
- Our usual response to stress
- How we organize thoughts, tasks, and stuff

The good news about habits comes from the study of the brain. Scientists have discovered that what happens in the brain when we do something repeatedly is that a pathway called a neural circuit is formed. This pathway gets stronger every time we think or do the same thing. Like a river cutting through a valley, the longer it flows in the same path, the deeper and stronger that path becomes. That is how habits are made. So all we have to do to create a new habit is to do something else repeatedly. Chances are you have heard the adage that it takes three weeks to create a habit. Science now has the evidence and the adage is close to true. It takes the brain three to six weeks to create strong new neural circuits, a new path for the river to take.

Do not spend a lot of time resisting an old pattern or trying to drop it. Brain research shows that focusing on something strengthens it—so it is better to put your energy into the new behavior.

Here is a super tip: simply thinking about the new habit (imagining it in your mind's eye and thinking of yourself already having it) helps build the new habit. So when you are committed to a new habit, spend a lot of time rehearsing it in your mind.

Use mental note taking to deal with feelings that threaten to derail you. If feelings of frustration, anger, annoyance, or fear knock you off balance, brain research offers this: Label what you are feeling. Saying, either silently or aloud, "I am nervous," or "I am frustrated," calms the brain so it can get back on track.

Sometimes we can develop new habits that get us what we want indirectly. An exercise habit can improve our health, a savings habit can finance a dream vacation, and building simple habits, like hugging six times a day, can enhance a marriage. (See *How to Improve Your Marriage Without Talking About It*, by Patricia Love and Steven Stosny.)

The best discovery of the recent research is that our brains have the ability to change dramatically—throughout our lives until the day we die. As simplistic as all this sounds, it is truly based on neuroscience—the study of how the brain works.

Coaching Tips and Questions

- Look at your habits of thought, attitude, and behavior. Which ones do you want to reinforce and which would you rather replace?
- What is a new thought or attitude habit you want to develop?
- What will you practice to make sure the habit sticks?
- What is a new behavior you want to cultivate?
- How can you see that the habit reroutes a river in your brain?
- Why not, as Aristotle suggested, make excellence a habit in your life?

1-5
Metaphors

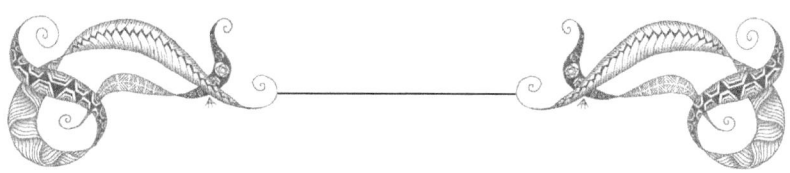

A picture is worth a thousand words.
– Unknown

METAPHORS ARE WORD PICTURES THAT ENGAGE the whole mind. They are grasped all at once instead of one piece at a time. They capture both facts and feelings. Metaphors and other word pictures have enormous power to help us understand things.

Examples

- A client of mine was part of a team asked to make budget decisions with incomplete information. He could not seem to find the right words to express his frustration. "Can you think of a metaphor?" I asked. He thought a minute and then smiled. "I'm with a group riding through a dark tunnel on bicycles. Only one person has a light on his bike, and it's not me." Bingo!

- On trying to change someone, Insoo Kim Berg said "If you rearrange someone's furniture uninvited, they'll put it all back when you leave."

Coaching Tips and Questions

When you are stuck or having trouble getting your point across, try the following:

- Paint a word picture or use a metaphor to describe the situation.

- If your metaphor or picture is not quite right, come up with another. Be creative. Metaphors can come from anywhere: nature, children, sports, animals, a discipline far from your own.

- Then ask how the metaphor sheds light on the dilemma or gives you clues about how to proceed.

1-6

WABI-SABI

Wabi-sabi emphasizes direct, intuitive insight into truth beyond all intellectual conception.
— Wikipedia

I LOVE TO LEARN ABOUT WORDS AND IDEAS in one language that do not translate easily into another. Often such words and ideas hold clues to worldviews in one culture that are uncommon in the other. Wabi-sabi is a Japanese concept without a clear English translation. Therefore, people talk around it, describing it in many ways. It refers to the beauty of things imperfect, impermanent, and incomplete. The beauty of things modest, humble, and unconventional. Some say "rustic" is the closest word we have in English.

Wabi-sabi embodies the idea of natural process, such as the beauty that comes to wood or leather as it ages. Wabi-sabi is about simplicity in both material things and insights. At the core of wabi-sabi is the importance of transcending usual ways of looking at and thinking about things, about existence.

When I try to grasp this wonderful concept, many images come to mind:

- Fall leaves—glorious and then blown away

- A not-quite-finished book
- Hal's 34 year old leather cap that is softened with age and molded perfectly to his head
- A wrinkled face
- Deep, heart-felt sadness
- A fading flower
- A spontaneous smile
- Sand castles

I am not at all sure I grasp the full import of this concept, but I think if I lived a wabi-sabi worldview, I would stay very much in the present. I would see the beauty in things and experiences, while not trying to hold onto them.

Coaching Tips and Questions

- Find four things today that are imperfect. Find the beauty in each.
- Embrace every beautiful moment or thing, even as it changes.
- Commit to a way of seeing the world that accepts what is.

1-7
NOVELTY

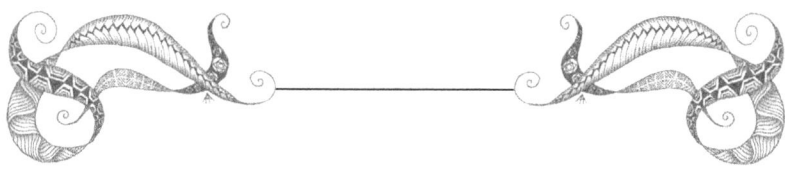

In order to keep the brain fit, we must learn something new, rather than simply replaying already-mastered skills.
– Michael Merzenich

A WONDERFUL VACATION IN San Miguel de Allende, Mexico, was a great experience of novelty for my husband, Hal, and me. San Miguel is high in the mountains of central Mexico, a gem of an old silver mining town, so charming that it has been named a National Monument. We left a chilly Pittsburgh, at 9 degrees Fahrenheit, and arrived to a clear 75 degrees in the Mexican mountains. Novelty was everywhere: cobblestone streets, brightly colored structures, flowering courtyards behind deceptively simple doorways, sounds of people speaking Spanish, children laughing, dogs barking, roosters crowing, and Mariachi music. The food delighted my taste buds. We walked miles, up and down the ragged streets and sidewalks, exchanging smiles and "Buenos Días" with the lovely Mexican people, speaking Spanish poorly and being forgiven on the spot, because we tried.

How the Brain Stays Young

Most people know that the brain is capable of making new cells and regenerating itself until the day we die. What people may not know is that people do not make brain cells at the same rate. One thing that seems to encourage the brain to make new cells, known as neurogenesis, is novelty.

It is almost funny how easy it is to stay in a rut. We want to try something new, learn something new, go somewhere new—yet it takes effort and can be a little scary, so often we do what we have always done instead. We want to start exercising, plan to start exercising, know how good it is to exercise, and yet we do not do it. The desire to be healthy and stay young can be strong, but so can the urge to sit on the couch or do what we have always done.

It motivates me to know that by stretching myself to learn new things and go new places I help my brain stay young and healthy. I came home from my trip to Mexico committed to studying Spanish. Learning a foreign language provides great novelty for the brain's benefit—both new words and new ways of thinking.

To Experience Novelty

- Change the pictures on the walls of your house.
- Drive to work or the store by different routes.
- Take a class in drawing or painting.
- Sleep on the other side of the bed.
- Try a new restaurant.
- Become proficient in using an electronic gadget or some challenging software.

COACHING TIPS AND QUESTIONS

- How can you put more novelty into your life? List five things.

- When, in the next week, will you try one of the five new things on your list?

- What can motivate you to learn new things, do new things, or go to new places?

1–8
LEARN AND FORGET

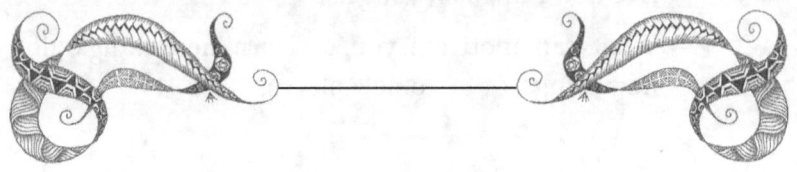

Learn all that stuff and then forget it.
— Miles Davis,
referring to the technical aspects of jazz

MILES DAVIS' QUOTE IS A GOOD WAY to describe the process of learning. I have heard it elaborated as four levels or stages:

LEVEL 1: UNCONSCIOUS INCOMPETENCE
We do not know what we do not know. We do not even know we do not know. This is true whether we are talking about eating healthily or playing jazz piano.

LEVEL 2: CONSCIOUS INCOMPETENCE
When we are new at some skill, we are often awkward. This is as true for eating healthily as it is for learning jazz improvisation.

LEVEL 3: CONSCIOUS COMPETENCE
We know it in our heads. We can eat well or play a beautiful jazz piece, but we have to pay good attention while we are doing it.

LEVEL 4: UNCONSCIOUS COMPETENCE
We do the thing without thinking. It feels automatic, whether it is eating well or rendering heartfelt jazz. This is the place where Miles Davis encourages us to "forget it." Stop thinking about it. Your bones know it now, so just BE it.

When my children were small, before every big learning leap, they were unusually crabby. I got so I expected something big and wonderful to happen when they were out of sorts for a week or more—and sure enough, there would be a breakthrough. They walked, talked, learned to read, ride a bike, type, play the flute, dance, and drive a car.

- Levels 1 to 3 are the "learn it" stages while Level 4 is the "forget it" stage.
- In Levels 1 and 4, we are happy—as in "ignorance is bliss."
- Levels 2 and 3 are often hard. That is where the crabbiness lives.

I had a big aha when I first heard of these steps in learning. It helps me be more patient with myself as I learn a new software application or become comfortable in a new culture.

Coaching Tips and Questions

- In your life, where are you on level 2 or 3 in terms of learning?
- How can your self-talk be more patient as you move toward level 4?

- With which people in your life might you be more patient and encouraging as they move through these stages?
- When will you start?

1-9
FORGETTING

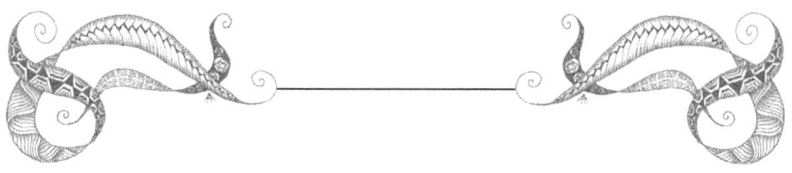

Not the power to remember, but it's very opposite, the power to forget, is a necessary condition for our existence.

– Sholem Asch

TOO MUCH REMEMBERING CAN BE A PROBLEM. If we remembered everything we learned every day, our minds would explode. In fact, this is just the trouble with some learning disabilities, where people do not know what to filter out, where and how to stay focused. On the other hand, think how important it is that we forget a slight or an act of unkindness, from someone. Too much remembering of emotional pain can keep us from enjoying the present or moving forward.

So—is it too much to extend this knowing—this valuing of the art of forgetting—to our aging selves? I forget many things these days: where I put important things, that I am supposed to call someone back, or the name of a character in a book I love. Sometimes I have the first letter, and the rest comes eight hours later. Then there is my dear friend who misplaced her phone and found it in the refrigerator. She did not forget where the phone is supposed to go—she was just distracted. I even made a spreadsheet to remember where I had stored some important things, like the vacuum cleaner instructions. Now I cannot find the spreadsheet! So imagine my delight when, while having a relaxed cup of coffee with my friend Astrid, I could not think of something I was trying to pull out of memory. Astrid would have none of my angst at not remembering.

"I think this forgetting is like a cleanly swept attic with a breeze blowing through," she offered. I immediately loved the metaphor and thought of my aging brain in this fresh, new way! The better to leave room for all the wisdom, right?

There are, of course, many things we are told to do to help keep the brain working well. Here are a few:

> MEDITATE
> I have been doing this every day and find it helps me stay relaxed and focused.
>
> PLAY BRAIN GAMES
> Include crossword puzzles and word games of all kinds, brain games online.
>
> EXERCISE
> Aerobic exercise 30 minutes, 4 to 5 times/week is great.
>
> LEARN SOMETHING NEW
> Learn a new skill, language, or recipe. I am taking painting lessons and I can FEEL my brain cells rearranging themselves!

I do not want you to think I am taking this too lightly. My dear husband Hal, who died in January 2012, had serious short-term memory loss in his last years. He was at first quite distressed. He DID many of the things listed above, which, I am convinced, slowed down his forgetting. Then he began to accept how unimportant many of the forgotten things were. He focused more on enjoying the moment!

On the way to accepting that some change is inevitable, it can be helpful to come up with reframes, metaphors like Astrid's, that allow us to see this forgetting thing in a more positive light. Almost everyone I know is working like crazy to get rid of the junk, or what is no longer useful in their homes. Maybe our brains are doing this for us, even while we sleep!

Coaching Tips and Questions

- How can you do everything possible to keep your brain sharp, while at the same time accepting that forgetting is a normal part of aging—not the end of the world?

- What metaphor can you create or embrace to remind yourself why it is important to be a good forgetter?

- In what ways is your self-talk about forgetting helping or hurting you?

1-10
QUESTIONS

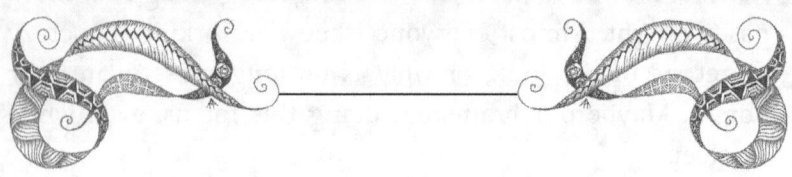

Answers stop thought.

– Larry Edelman

MOST OF US ARE VERY FOCUSED on solving problems, answering questions, and moving on. We measure our effectiveness by our ability to do so quickly. The downside is that as soon as we solve something, we stop thinking about it.

Here's the truth: Questions are often more powerful than answers. If we stay with a question, let it play in our minds, have conversations about it with others, find deeper questions beneath the first one, the eventual solution is richer and more sustainable than our first quick answer.

When you're struggling to solve a problem or answer important questions, go deeper: Aim for the question behind the question. For example, say you have a conflict with someone in an important relationship. Instead of asking, "How can I change his/her mind?" ask, "What do I really want?" "What do I suppose he/she really wants?" "Is there some way of getting what we both want without changing the other person?"

This is a difficult shift. But it is worth the effort. Often the edge an excellent leader has over a good leader is the ability to formulate great questions.

Coaching Tips and Questions

Practice formulating and asking "big questions" at work and at home. Consider starting with a few of these:

- What assumptions am I making?
- What other problem is related to this one? What is the relationship between the two?
- What question, if I knew its answer, would solve my stickiest problem?
- How do I contribute to what I don't like at work? At home?
- What does success look like for me?
- What gives me energy?
- What drains me?
- What if I'm wrong?
- What contribution would I really like to make?
- How might this problem look from a totally different perspective (the customer's, 10,000 feet in the air, 5 years into the future)?

1~11

INTENTION VS. EXPECTATION

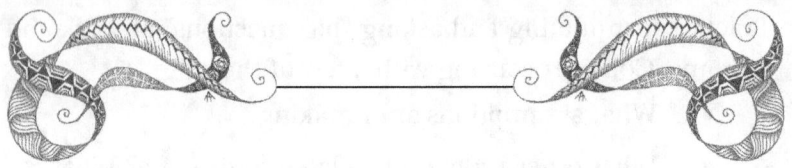

Expectation causes disappointment. Intention causes inspiration, direction, and commitment.
             - Qigong Master Mingtong Gu

THE DIFFERENCE BETWEEN INTENTION AND EXPECTATION may seem subtle. But it is huge.

When I stay focused on my intention, I feel empowered and energized. When I focus instead on my expectation, I often lose energy and feel disappointed and hopeless. Here's a small example. I agreed to drive my friend Shalla several blocks to work Friday morning because it was minus 6 degrees, and she has no car. Since I hated thinking of her walking to work in those conditions, I was happy to drive her. Yet when I flashed on my expectation, I felt scared and helpless. "It's icy," said the voice in my head. "This will be very hard. It could be dangerous." When I switched back and held tightly to my intention, it was simple. I plotted the flattest route and focused on getting Shalla safely to work, and it was easy.

Master Mingtong Gu says, "Intention is profoundly different from expectation. The difference can be illustrated in the analogy of climbing a mountain." He goes on to flesh out the analogy. Your intention is to go to the top of the mountain. Wherever you are at each moment, you know you're headed in the right direction. You don't get confused by the different views on the way, or the path dipping downward for a moment, because your intention is clear. You overcome whatever obstacles occur. If you're expecting to get to the top, and even expecting it will be a certain experience on the way, whenever the view or the obstacle is different, you may lose energy, feel discouraged, start blaming even. You might create stories around your emotion. "They should have warned me it might rain. I didn't expect all these rocks."

One place this distinction between intentions and expectations plays out is in relationships, both personal and professional. When we intend a relationship to work, we sign on to help achieve that outcome. If we expect some particular words or behavior from the other person, we set ourselves up for disappointment. We have no control over the other. We simply cannot change other people, as hard as we may try. But we all do have expectations, including some we're unaware of. These often live in the form of what we think others "should" do.

A small example illustrates how holding fast to intentions can help us be creative in the face of dashed expectations. For years, my husband, Gene, and I accompanied each other to our respective employers' holiday parties. Then one year the parties were on the same night, in far-apart locations. When we discovered this, we were both upset. The thought of going without the other was hard; skipping one party or the other felt impossible. For a while we were stuck. Then, remembering our biggest intention—to make our relationship work—we set out to find a solution that would honor that intention. So I asked Gene, "On a scale from 1 to 10, how important is it for you that I come to your party with you?" He said, "10." He asked me the same. I was surprised to realize, my need for him to be with me at this particular party was only a two or three. Quickly we formed a plan where we went together to his party, then I left alone for my party. I share my trivial story because it became a model for us in other situations.

Intentions	Expectations
I am engaged and have responsibility	I have little control, waiting for others or circumstances to deliver
I learn on the path—about myself, others, life	I develop stories—often emotional—about my experience of not getting what I expected
I am encouraged by my progress	I am discouraged by distractions, views
Remembering my intention, I am empowered, energized	Discouraged by all the views, I feel powerless, victimized

Holding onto the bigger intention, we can learn from any experiences that are unexpected, clear any obstacles. The intention is the guiding light. Letting go of expectations produces the best result.

Coaching Tips and Questions

- Think of a relationship or situation that is problematic to you in some way.
- What is your deepest intention there?
- What expectations get in the way of your intention?

- How can you hold onto the intention and drop the expectations?
- When will you do that?

1~12
DEVELOPING IDEAS

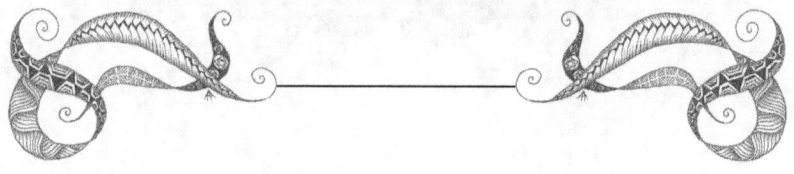

An idea can turn to dust or magic, depending on the talent that rubs against it.
— William Bernbach

IN MY EXPERIENCE, good ideas are almost always improved by sharing.

The Bahá'í Faith uses group consultation as its primary decision-making process. An important part of the practice is that as soon as an idea is expressed, it belongs to the group. The group may accept or reject the idea, modify or refine it. The originator has no need to defend it or take responsibility for it. This is a very freeing practice.

Imagine how things might change if this were a widespread practice. What if people in business and politics didn't get attached to their ideas but trusted the process of honing an idea together for the greater good? Imagine how productive it might be if we could do this with loved ones as well. Not my idea or yours, but one that emerges when we put our ideas together and then play with them, as an artist does with clay, to see what works best for us.

For example, when I headed a team, I often presented a proposal for some project to the team. Even when my idea was good, it was always improved by the input of others. Sometimes I was amazed at the result. Frequently the ideas we adopted in the end didn't resemble my original proposal at all. I would ask myself, "Why didn't I think of that?" The answer, I think, is that I am only one brain. My idea needed more "talent" to "rub against it," as Bernbach says.

When I moved into my current home, I went shopping for a sofa. I took a piece of graph paper with me on which I'd marked the dimensions of the living room, and a little cut-out piece for a sofa. I was talking to a decorator/saleswoman, when another person overheard us and came to look. She glanced at my little picture and suggested, "Why don't you move your front door? Your living room would suddenly become much bigger." It seemed outlandish; I thought it would be too expensive. But the idea played in my mind. Long story short, I did it. It was not expensive, and it improved the house immensely. Not in a hundred years would I have thought to move the front door!

Coaching Tips and Questions

- What idea are you playing with that might be improved by sharing it?
- Who could help you develop the idea?
- When will you start?

1-13

Make Mistakes

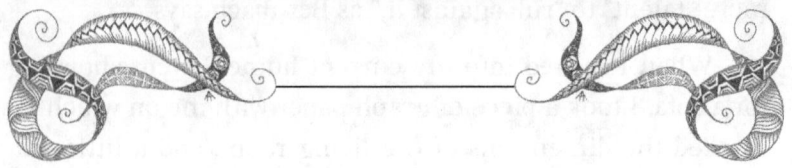

The only real mistake is the one from which we learn nothing.

– John Powell

I HAVE NO IDEA IF I MAKE MORE MISTAKES than most people—but I sure make a lot of them!

Examples

- Recently I was getting gas at the BP, and I ran into the store to buy a gallon of milk. I came back to my car and drove away, forgetting the nozzle was still in the car. When someone started honking, I was oblivious. A kind woman knocked on my window to let me know the honker was trying to tell me I'd driven away from the pump still hooked up! Luckily, when I returned to the pump, nothing was hurt. I was just embarrassed.
- Once, when my husband Hal and I were shopping, he grabbed a large carton of cottage cheese and it got away from him, plummeting to the floor with a splat. I flagged down a store employee and told him we'd had a cottage cheese accident. He looked at Hal, who had cottage cheese on his jacket,

glove, and shoe, and said, "I can see who is responsible." Hal said, "Mistakes were made." The friendly man jokingly threatened to clean it up with Hal's hat.

- Many years ago, I led a large drug and alcoholic treatment center into becoming totally smoke-free. The health dangers of tobacco had been proven, and many of our patients smoked. It was an eminently reasonable thing to do. We had treated too many people who got sober, only to die of a nicotine-related illness. But we made mistakes. Some of our staff still smoked, in spite of assisted attempts to quit. The patients developed a black market in cigarettes. Many potential patients refused to come to our center. After nine months, it became clear that if we wanted to continue with our primary mission of treating drug and alcohol addicts, we had to modify our hard no-smoking stance. So we did.

I like Richard Needham's perspective: "Strong people make as many mistakes as weak people. Difference is that strong people admit their mistakes, laugh at them, learn from them. That is how they become strong."

Coaching Tips and Questions

- Dare to try things, knowing you will inevitably make mistakes.
- Remember that mistakes are human. When you make one, laugh, forgive yourself, and move on.
- Acknowledge your mistakes.
- Learn from your mistakes whenever possible.

- Remember the old adage, "Mistakes are stepping stones to success."

1-14

GO TO THE BALCONY

Go to the balcony.
— William Ury

ACCORDING TO William Ury, going to the balcony is a way to collect your wits in the midst of conflict, to distance yourself from your natural impulses and emotions. If you mentally go to the balcony—actually picture yourself walking up the steps to a balcony—and look down on the stage of any troublesome situation, you see a bigger picture. Musashi, the great samurai, called this "a distanced view of close things."

When you're looking down from the balcony, you can often get above the emotions of the moment and see the relatedness of the parts, including yourself! When you're looking at the big picture, it is easier to see that when something changes in one part of the picture, it affects the other parts.

Going to the balcony is valuable for individuals, families, organizations, companies, and nations. Going to the balcony can:

- Buy time

- Allow you to see the bigger system, or systems within systems
- Help you consider both intended and unintended consequences of any action you may take

Coaching Tips and Questions

- Think of one situation or challenge that is currently bothering you. Try going to the balcony in relation to it. What patterns do you see? How is your response helping or hurting the situation?
- Get in the habit of going to the balcony to help understand and resolve sticky issues. It is a metaphorical way to expand your perspective, literally.
- Learn more by reading William Ury's book, *Getting Past No, Negotiating Your Way from Confrontation to Cooperation.*

1-15

DECISION MAKING

No trumpets sound when the important decisions of our life are made. Destiny is made known silently.
– Agnes de Mille

BIG DECISIONS ARE SOMETIMES EASY AND SOMETIMES agonizingly difficult!

I am comforted by research proving that in addition to the brain in our head, we have brain cells in both our hearts and our guts to help us make decisions. These multiple brains work on our decisions not only when we're focused on the goals, but also when we're goofing off and when we're asleep.

Here are four sure-fire, slightly unusual methods for use in any decision-making process. They'll help you decide how to handle a sticky situation at home or work, whether or not to make a commitment to a person, a project, an investment, or what kind of vacation to take.

1. DIFFERENT THINKING PERSPECTIVES
   Use Herrmann's whole brain model to make sure you're looking at the choices from different thinking perspectives. Herrmann identifies four quadrants in the brain. According to his Whole

Brain Technology, those four quadrants are the analyzing brain, the organizing brain, the feeling brain, and the imagining brain. Each of us prefers to use one or more of these parts of our brain more than the others. The strongest decisions, though, seem to come from considering things from all four perspectives. To get that perspective, we can walk around the four quadrants by asking these questions:
- Do I have all the facts?
- Will I be in control?
- How will this decision affect others?
- Have I seen all the hidden possibilities?

2. IMAGINE IN VIVID DETAIL
When deciding between two options, spend time imagining in vivid detail that you've committed to choice A. Notice your thoughts and feelings. Are you happy? Relieved? Tense? Sad? Then switch and imagine vividly that you have committed to choice B. Ask the same questions. Go back and forth several times. The decision will often make itself.

3. BE CLEAR ABOUT WHAT YOU WANT
Ask yourself, "What do I want? What do I really, really want? And what do I NOT want?" We often try to make decisions on the merits of the options without being clear first about what we want.

4. LEVERAGE YOUR SUBCONSCIOUS
If you are having trouble making a decision, just before you go to sleep, give it to your subconscious to work on while you sleep. Don't be surprised when a dream provides clear direction or you wake up with the decision made.

Coaching Tips and Questions

- Consider the four decision-making strategies described above.
- Choose one and try it in a situation where you need to make a decision.
- If one doesn't work well, try another.

1~16
INVENT A BETTER STORY

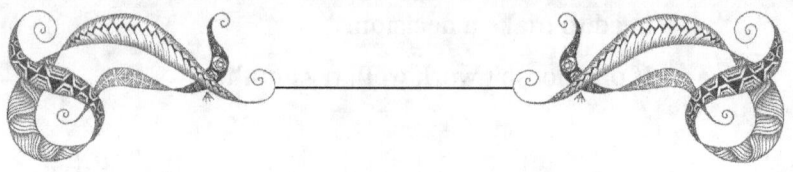

We are what we think. With our thoughts we make the world.

— Buddha

WE ALL INVENT STORIES TO EXPLAIN THE WORLD to ourselves.

Isn't it interesting that we make up different stories for the same events? Some of us make up stories about evil empires to explain the events of 9/11; some make up stories with jealousy of the American way of life at their core. Others make up stories of protest against the globalization of U.S. culture.

Many things—including our culture, experience, and habits of thinking—influence the stories we make up. Since we're just making sense of our experience, we aren't usually aware we're making up stories. We don't realize we could make up better ones.

Examples

- Your doctor leaves you a message on Friday saying he wants to talk to you about your test results on Monday. You can make up a story
    - of your own impending, slow, painful death, or
    - about how the lab lost your blood and needs a new sample.
- A friend is acting distant. You can make up a story
    - that she is mad at you, or
    - that she's struggling with something totally unrelated to you and will tell you about it soon.
- You don't hear back quickly from a job interview. You can make up a story
    - that they didn't like you, or
    - that their focus got pulled somewhere else and the hiring process has been delayed.

Making up good stories is not the same as rationalizing or lying to yourself. If you get bad news or something painful is going on, you need to face it.

But when there is uncertainty, when you really don't know what's going on with a person or situation, you can make up any story you want. And it's easier to live through the uncertainty when you make up a good story. Just practicing making up better stories can be both calming and entertaining.

Coaching Tips and Questions

- Where in your current life would you like to have a better story?
- Think of two better stories. Choose whichever one you like best.

1-17

INSPIRATION

Aerodynamically, the bumblebee shouldn't be able to fly, but the bumblebee doesn't know it so it goes on flying anyway.

– Mary Kay Ash

I LIKE FEELING INSPIRED. The dictionary describes the state of being inspired this way: "aroused, animated, or imbued with the spirit to do or be something, by or as if by supernatural or divine influence." Because I like this state, I've always started each day reading something inspiring. When my husband, Hal, was alive, we read a couple of inspirational writings together and talked about them each morning. What a wonderful way to start the day.

I once attended a conference that was over-the-top inspiring. It was The Bigger Game Expo (www.Bigger Game.com) in Silver Bay, NY. Rick Tamlyn, who co-wrote a book, *The Bigger Game*, gathered 17 people to tell their stories of playing a bigger game, surprising even themselves by what they'd done and who they'd become. The diversity in these stories was one of the most beautiful aspects of the conference. I'd love to describe every one of them, but I'll choose a few and hope they convey even a fraction of the inspiration that came through in person.

Anita Kruse

Founder & Executive Director of Purple Songs Can Fly (www.PurpleSongsCanFly.org). Anita created the first recording studio ever on a pediatric cancer floor at Texas Children's Cancer and Hematology Centers. The children work with Anita to write and record their own songs. They are then able to share their music with family and friends on CD recordings. This program has inspired similar programs across the country.

The Yaari brothers, Ronen and Eyal

They describe an amazing journey that unfolded after their ideal lives were interrupted by personal loss, Parkinson's, and heart disease. The brothers and Ronen's 13-year-old son, Oren, hit the road in an epic bid to transform their challenges into personal triumphs. In the process, they discovered how to empower each other. Their bike ride across Israel on a specially made tandem bicycle (that allowed Ronen to do the heavy lifting for Eyal, who has Parkinson's disease) is so touching you should buy the video, *The Power of Bro* (www.PowerOfBro.com).

Lynne Twist (www.LynneTwist.com)

Lynne is a global activist and author who, at an early age, committed herself to ending world hunger. On that journey, she has met and worked with amazing people like Mother Teresa, raised millions of dollars for the cause, and raised a family in the context of a "committed life." Her most recent work, known as The Pachamama Alliance (www.Pachamama.org), is committed to "bringing forth an environmentally sustainable, spiritually fulfilling, socially just human presence on this planet." She has such an authentic presence, humble, real, and powerful, that I wept listening to her.

Alice Coles

She was invited to this conference to receive an award for her bigger game. You may have seen Alice on 60 minutes in 2004. This unlikely leader spearheaded the effort to defeat a plan by the State of Virginia to build a maximum-security prison in her community of Bayview. Bayview was a forgotten place, an African-American community of dilapidated wooden shacks with no running water, central heating, or indoor toilets. After rising to fend off the prison bid, community members asked, "If we could do that—why are we living wretched like this?" Alice said, "Let's go home and carry this energy, pool it together and help ourselves." They went on to raise $10 million, built dozens of new homes, a water treatment plant, and a laundry facility. Residents continue to improve the community every day. Alice and her daughter Niketa are eloquent and gently powerful!

At this conference, I felt the strong call to continue committing my life to helping people improve their relationships. Then there was a bonus inspiration for me. The attendees, from many countries, were often as inspiring as the presenters were. One day after lunch, Paul Smith began to play his Native American flute. The music touched my soul. After I found he'd only been playing a few months, I decided to get and learn to play one. I found a flute maker who was a very generous spirit, talked with him on the phone, heard his flutes, and bought one. I am learning to cover the holes well so the notes aren't squeaky, and every now and then, I get a glimpse of how glorious this music can be.

Coaching Tips and Questions

- What inspires you?
- How can you get more inspiration in your life?
  - Books?
  - Movies?
  - Quotes?
  - Music?
  - Art?
  - Video clips?
- How can you spend more time with people who inspire you?
- How can you cut down on what saps energy?
  - Less news?
  - Less time with people who tend to be negative?
- When will you establish a regular practice to keep the inspiration coming in?
  - Reading something inspirational every morning?
  - Evening?

Chapter 2

Create Relationships That Work

CREATE RELATIONSHIPS THAT WORK

They may forget what you said but they will never forget how you made them feel.

– Carl Buehner

RELATIONSHIPS ARE AT THE CENTER OF OUR LIVES. There are the relationships we have, ones we wish we had, ones we wish we didn't have, can't live with, and can't live without. There are harmonious relationships, contentious relationships, and many that are both. For example, we have nice neighbors who let their dogs bark all day (or night). We find a partner and then sometimes wonder why we ever thought this partnership was a good idea. We have adorable babies who grow up to be people with ideas of their own. Sometimes those ideas mesh with ours, and sometimes they horrify us.

Most people will tell you that relationships are their greatest source of joy and pain, pleasure and tension.

In my work as a coach, people tell me repeatedly that difficulties with people are the most draining part of their work. Even loners are in relationship all the time—wondering how to keep people at bay, how to avoid meetings, or live with a minimum of interaction.

Some of our relationships are with people we don't choose: family members, new neighbors, and people at work. Others are relationships we choose, like partners and friends. It is interesting to notice the similarities in those we choose and don't choose.

Whether at work or at home, relationships, and how we handle them, have a major impact on the quality of our lives. When we figure out how to live in relationships better—at work and at home—the whole world is improved!

The good news is that we can have relationships that work. Really well! All the time! But here's the rub: We almost always think it's the other person who needs to change for the relationship to improve. The hard news is that we're the ones who have to change, but not in the ways we might think or might have already tried.

We have absolutely no control over other people, even when we think we do. We can't make people do what we want them to do—not even our children, our spouse, or our employees. We might get others to comply for a while. But if we've forced them to shift their behavior, it won't last. In fact, the coercion we exert will probably come back to haunt us.

How then do we live happily in relationship? How can relationships stop bothering us, and waking us up at night? What can we do? Answers to those questions are at the heart of this section. And that's a pun of sorts, because the key is the condition of OUR hearts. I invite you to consider the essays in this section with an open heart, one willing to see things from a new perspective—and even to change. Your life will be better for it.

2-1

Relationships

The quality of your life is determined by the quality of your relationships.

– Henry Mackay

The opening quote from a class I took from the Arbinger Institute went like this, "Think of three people in your life with whom you'd like to improve your relationship. Now ask yourself honestly: How do you cause trouble for each of them?" To me it was a shocking question! I had thought a lot about how each of my chosen three troubled me but very little about how I troubled them. Thinking seriously about this was an eye-opener. I could actually imagine how my judgments and sense of superiority probably felt to them.

The Arbinger model maintains that it's our "way of being" with people that determines the quality of the relationship. "Way of being" is deeper than behavior. Here's what that means: If we are angry with someone but act sweetly, that person is not fooled. If we are indifferent to someone but feign interest, that person feels our disinterest.

The recommendation is that we see people—all people—as people instead of objects. This includes people we love, people we don't care for, and people we meet casually, like clerks and flight attendants.

The Arbinger model suggests that the three most common ways we see people as objects are when we see them as:

- Obstacles
- Vehicles
- Irrelevancies

In contrast, when we see people as people, we recognize they have hopes, dreams, and burdens of their own, that their behavior makes some kind of sense to them, even if we don't see it. It means taking the time and making the effort to listen to people openly, with—as the Arbinger model says—a "heart of peace" instead of a "heart of war." When we have a "heart of peace" toward someone, we respond to that person instead of reacting. Relationships in which we maintain a "heart of peace" are good even if there are significant differences between us or we need to say difficult things.

The remarkable thing I've noticed is that when people prioritize relationships, work to maintain a "heart of peace," and see people as people, the rest of their lives take care of themselves. They are often highly successful at whatever they do.

Coaching Tips and Questions

- Name three people with whom you'd like to improve your relationship. How might each of these people feel to be on the receiving end of you?
- How are you trouble to each of these people?
- Do you see any of these people as objects? Obstacles, vehicles, irrelevancies?

- What do you see if you look carefully at each of them as a person? What are their hopes, dreams, and burdens?
- What would it mean to have a "heart of peace" toward each of these people?
- To learn more about the Arbinger model, visit www.arbinger.com and read *Leadership and Self Deception* and *The Anatomy of Peace*, books written by The Arbinger Institute.

2-2
INTERDEPENDENCE

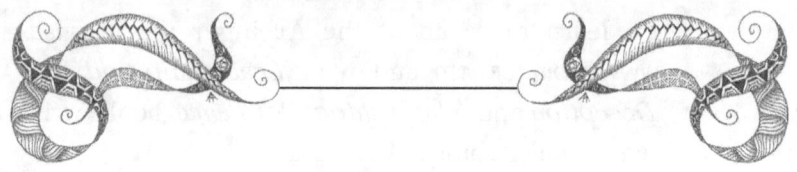

We are here to awaken from the illusion of our separateness.

– Thich Nhat Hanh

IF THE QUOTE IS CORRECT, AND WE ARE NOT SEPARATE, we must be linked, even interdependent! I find the notion of interdependence both attractive and scary. The dictionary defines interdependence in a couple of ways:

1. Depending on each other: unable to exist or survive without each other
2. Relying on mutual assistance, support, cooperation, or interaction among parts or members

I'm attracted because I like thinking that cooperation and service to each other is the way we'll thrive as a species; maybe it's even the requirement for continued existence. There is an old saying, "When someone in a family breaks a toe, the whole family limps." I know the truth of this because when someone I love is suffering, I hurt.

I also know about interdependence in my body. When my tooth aches, the rest of me doesn't feel well either. The scary part is that if we are not separate, but all of us are interdependent, what about the drunk who's yelling epithets on the street corner? What about the mother I saw strike her child in the grocery store parking lot? I want to separate myself from these folks; something in me recoils at the idea that I'm interdependent with them.

In *Glimpse After Glimpse, Daily Reflections on Living and Dying*, Sogyal Rinpoche says,

> *If we are interdependent with everything and everyone, even our smallest, least significant thought, word, and action have real consequences throughout the universe.*
>
> *Throw a pebble into a pond. It sends a shiver across the surface of the water. Ripples merge into one another and create new ones. Everything is inextricably interrelated. We come to realize that we are responsible for everything we do, say, or think, responsible in fact for ourselves, everyone and everything else, and the entire universe.*

Coaching Tips and Questions

The idea of interdependence is hard to understand, let alone embrace. But just pretend for a minute that it's true, that we are inextricably connected to everything else and that our thoughts and deeds have real consequences in the world. Stop and get inside that belief for just a minute, then answer these questions from there:

- How might you think differently?
- What might you say differently?
- How might you spend your time?
- How might you experience your responsibility to other people?
- How might you use earth's resources differently (air, water, fuel, etc.)?

- What else might you do differently?
- Keep pondering this possibility. Interdependence just might be true.

2-3
LISTENING

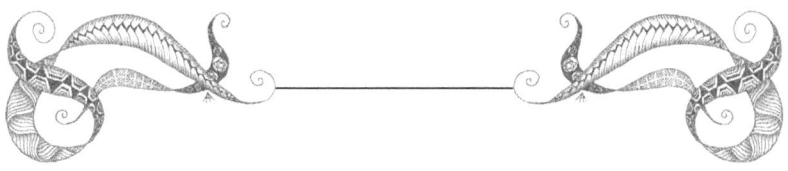

I know that you believe you understand what you think I said.
— Robert McCloskey

TO LISTEN WELL IS TO STILL OUR MINDS, loosen our perspectives, and open our hearts. Are you a good listener?

When we listen and do something else at the same time, the speaker often feels slighted. When my daughter Lisa was young, she would go to the Sunday movie and come home excited to tell me about it. I'd listen as I cooked or did some other thing, trying to stay interested by asking a question or injecting a comment. She'd say, "I think you're not listening. Maybe stop what you're doing so you can hear better." What I missed was that she was giving me herself—her feelings, her response to things, her view of the world.

Many years ago I was about to go on a trip to Israel. My friend Sandra said, "When you get back, come and really tell me about it, every little detail. I will listen happily for hours." What an invitation! And I did. I told story after story while she listened. Her listening was an enormous gift to me. She smiled as I left, thanking me genuinely for "a visit to Israel."

Learning About Listening From The Deaf

Ironically, a profound insight into good listening comes from the deaf. Bruno Kahne, a senior consultant at Airbusiness Academy, was developing a leadership program for Airbus. There he met an executive whose youngest son was born without hearing. Through this connection, Kahne became familiar with the culture of the deaf, their visual, intensely expressive language. He realized that many deaf people have developed communication skills more thoroughly than hearing people, which make them uncommonly effective at getting their point across. In a radical experiment, he began using deaf people as communication consultants for corporate clients. Some of the simple, but oft-ignored lessons for good listening that came from the deaf are:

- Look people in the eye
- Don't interrupt
- Say what you mean, as simply as possible
- When you don't understand something, ask
- Stay focused

Coaching Tips and Questions

- How often do you listen as recommended above by the deaf?
- How do you pay more attention to the other person than to the voices in your own head?
- How do you listen to what is not being said?
- In what spirit do you listen?
    - To get an answer?
    - To learn?
    - To argue?

- What can you decide not to listen to?
  - The news?
  - Gossip?
  - Advertising?
  - Your negative, inner voice?
- What person in your life do you feel moved to listen to more fully?

2-4
WALK A MILE

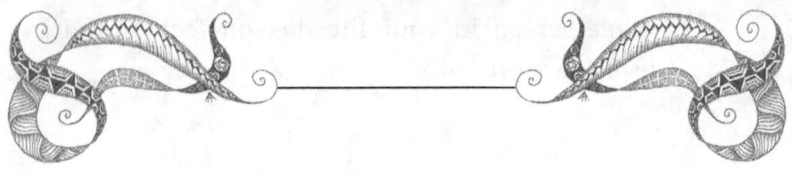

Never judge a person until you have walked a mile in his shoes.

– Old adage

WHEN MY SON GORDON WAS JUST PAST TWO YEARS OLD, we moved into a house on Beeler St. My husband and I were poor graduate students and our kids slept on mattresses on the floor. The window in their room was near the street; the traffic sounds were loud.

Gordon began waking up in the middle of a nap or the middle of the night, wailing, "The Volkswagen is coming, the Volkswagen is coming!" He was inconsolable. He was sure a Volkswagen was going to come in the window and run over him. We assured him gently that cars don't come into houses. We told him a car wouldn't fit through the window. My husband got a measuring tape and measured first the window and then the neighbor's Volkswagen to show Gordon how foolish were his fears. None of our efforts helped.

One day Gordon and I were playing in his room. I was lying on his bed. He said, "You're a baby," so I said, "You're a mommy." He was delighted. I began to cry out, "The Volkswagen is coming, the Volkswagen is coming!" He quickly reassured me, saying, "Don't worry, baby, I'll push it out." And he went to the window and pushed. Later, when he woke up terrified, I calmly repeated his words, "Don't worry, I'll push it out." I went to the window and pushed. His terror stopped.

I love remembering that story. It is fascinating on many levels, and I yearn to plumb its meaning. But remember, his father and I were both graduate students in psychology. We'd already tried everything we could think of to calm him. It was only when I invited Gordon to walk in MY shoes that he taught us how to be helpful!

When I worked in the drug and alcohol treatment field, therapists were annoyed that the accounting office always seemed to be haranguing them for this or that piece of information. For their part the accounting office had trouble understanding how therapists spent their time—it seemed as if they just talked with patients, and how hard could that be? A program allowing each to shadow the other for several hours had remarkable results. Therapists developed new appreciation for how key their information was to the accounting process. Accounting staff developed new respect for the seriousness of the entire project of rehabilitation and the skill required by therapists to help patients.

On several occasions when men have complained to me that their wives don't do anything—just stay home and take care of kids—I have prescribed that the men stay home one entire day and find out what their wives do. Usually the men are exhausted and eager to return to their own jobs.

How do you walk in another's shoes or imagine another person's experience? One good way is to ask. John, a coaching client of mine, assumed one of his staff members was sabotaging his leadership by not showing up for early morning teleconferences with global partners. I suggested

John ask him what was going on. To John's amazement, he found the teleconferences prevented his employee from driving to work with the carpool he had organized and taking his daughter to school. They worked out a mutually agreeable compromise.

Walking in another's shoes is such a cliché that we may not notice how profound it is. Walking in another's shoes can change your perspective, expand your understanding, and increase your empathy. As in the situation with Gordon, it can also solve difficult problems. Imagine what might happen if people were able to walk in each other's shoes when there were serious political or religious differences. Perhaps we would more quickly become citizens of one world.

Coaching Tips and Questions

- When you have difficulty with a family member, friend or employee, imagine walking a mile in that person's shoes.
- Figure out a creative way, as two-year-old Gordon did, to invite someone to walk in your shoes.
- When you find yourself judging another, imagine what it might be like to BE that person.

2-5
FROM BLAME TO ACCOUNTABILITY

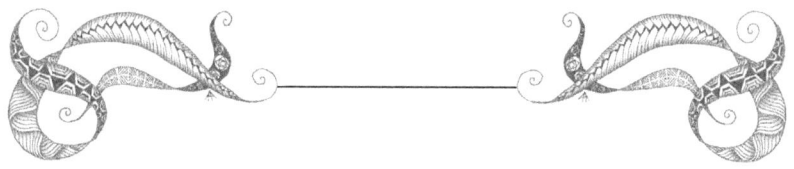

Blame is like sugar; it produces a brief boost and then a let down.
— Marilyn Paul

JAMIE, MY BARELY TWO-YEAR-OLD GRANDDAUGHTER, knocked important things off a table. "Meow did it," she said, referring to her stuffed cat.

How easily we fall into blaming each other in families and in organizations. We form blame-based communities by playing what Lois Perelman calls PEANUT:

    P= take a *position*

    E= gather *evidence*

    A= find people who *agree* with you; then run

    N= *non-*

    U= *useful-*

    T= *tapes*

The trouble with blaming is that when we blame, we don't learn. Blame breeds fear and distrust. When we create a blaming culture, there is little room for progress, and success is unlikely.

Here are two examples of how you or someone else might play PEANUT.

1. You decide your new neighbor is a bit strange. Your spouse agrees. You ask another neighbor if he's noticed this strangeness. He says, "Yes," and adds some things you missed. You laugh together. You watch for evidence and share it with a widening circle of neighbors.

2. You and your fellow workers think the top management is incompetent. You watch for their missteps. Then you find people who agree, and in the cafeteria or the bathroom, you share your evidence. You roll your eyes, shake your head, throw up your hands. You had similar conversations yesterday and will have similar conversations tomorrow. At the moment, it feels good. But over time, it becomes a negative spiral and drains your energy.

Playing PEANUT helps us feel like part of the "in crowd." The trouble is it also gets and keeps us stuck in a negative rut.

There are many ways to get out of the PEANUT rut. Here are a few:

- Stop playing PEANUT, period. In any new relationship (individual or group), have a clarifying conversation at the outset. Spell out assumptions, expectations, time-lines. Pre-plan what you will do when problems develop.

- Next time someone brings you Evidence and looks for your Agreement on some Position you've both taken, tell her you're experimenting with a different way of looking at things.

- Begin to notice and appreciate even the smallest positive thing that comes from top management (or your spouse, neighbor, colleague, child, or whomever is the subject of your PEANUT).

- Share your positive observation with anyone who brings you Evidence.

- Have "accountability conversations" periodically as a way to keep the relationship free from blame. These don't just happen. SCHEDULE them with your important partners, both personal and work related. When the shared goal of such conversations is success for all parties and the joint project, they can make a powerful difference.

Try these steps both at work and at home. You will be amazed at how much better everything works when you switch from blaming to accountability.

Coaching Tips and Questions

- With whom do you play PEANUT?
- Which suggestions above could help you stop?
- How much better would you feel without the negative energy of an active PEANUT game?
- What step will you take this week to stop blaming?

2-6
DIFFERENCES AND CURIOSITY

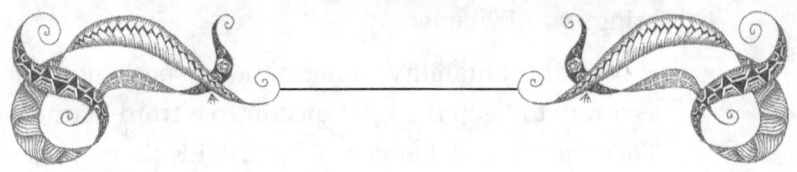

All the world is strange
Except thee and me
And sometimes I even wonder about thee.
— Unknown

PEOPLE ARE AMAZINGLY DIFFERENT FROM EACH OTHER. This is so obvious it is a cliché. Still, the simple notion is profound. People ARE different. It's differences among us that lead to frustration and fighting and divorce and war. The differences come in many forms. Here are a few:

- How we think
- What we find easy to do
- How we process and express emotion
- The people we like
- How we communicate
- What really matters to us
- What we find beautiful, inspiring, interesting
- The color and texture of our skin and hair
- What we find fun and funny

DNA evidence shows that humans differ in less than one percent of their total genetic code. So many important parts of us are the same: our need for food, water, shelter, love, and belonging. This is quite amazing when you think of how much time and energy we spend reacting to differences.

Perhaps when we accept our differences we can appreciate how similar we are and become more peaceful.

Coaching Tips and Questions

Instead of getting mad at differences, get curious. Whether the difference is with a single loved one or a group, see it as a puzzle. Investigate. Question yourself and the other about assumptions, history, how the world looks from that other vantage point. Research by reading things you wouldn't usually read. Then, use your findings to do one of these:

- Honor the difference.
- Celebrate the difference.
- Hire people who like to do what you don't like doing.
- Oppose a position effectively by understanding it.
- Focus on how life is richer because of differences.
- Notice how solutions are stronger when they embrace differences.

2-7

CONFLICT

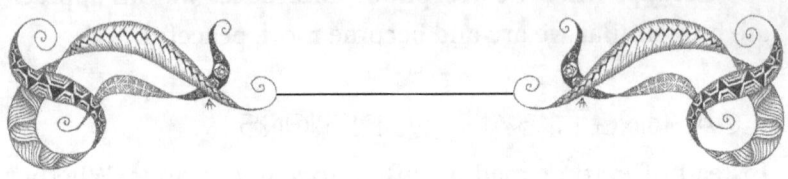

In conflict, be fair and generous.

— Tao te Ching

SONYA, A COACHING CLIENT, TOLD ME that her family's Thanksgiving was ruined by a big blowup she had with her brother, Doug. "He is so bullheaded," she said. "He was just asking for it. I felt as if I didn't have a choice."

Sonya genuinely wanted to see another way she could have handled the situation because she loves her family and would be with them again at Christmas. Her fight with Doug put a damper on everyone's holiday, which she regretted.

It turns out that the trigger for Sonya and Doug was a difference in political view. She is liberal and he is very taken with the Tea Party. (In how many Thanksgiving dining rooms did this drama play out?)

On reflection, Sonya realized she had arrived at the gathering ready to pick a fight with Doug, knowing it would happen. In fact, she started it, with what she meant to sound like a tease. But her comment was really a nasty dig. She was hurt by some of what Doug said, but said she would not have wanted to be on the receiving end of herself. She got mean, bringing up things from the past, embarrassing him in front of the whole family. Then she carefully recruited her sister to her side, while an uncle enlisted on Doug's side. It became all-out war.

Softening

I asked Sonya if she had any fond memories of Doug as a child. She softened, got quiet, and told me that he'd been her favorite sibling. Close in age, they'd both been adventurous and had climbed trees together and walked in the creek near their house. They once built an amazing fort high in a tree. She had taught Doug to read before he was five, and the two of them were the readers in the family. She missed that closeness.

From that softer place, Sonya was also able to say that she'd been impressed and delighted at what a patient and attentive dad Doug was to his 8-month-old son, Dylan. She suspected that Doug's wish was much like hers, in truth, to be close to his family—including her.

At the end of our session, I asked Sonya what she felt she might do for Doug. She said she wanted to send him an e-mail reminiscing about how much fun they'd had together as kids playing in the woods. She was even going to attach a picture of the tree fort that she'd recently scanned. She'd tell him what a good dad he is and how cute Dylan is. She'd apologize for her bullheadedness and suggest they agree in advance not to talk politics at Christmas because she loved him too much to let their political differences polarize the family.

Once we remember the humanity in the other, our hearts can soften. From this softened place, we can see that we DO have a choice. We can be fair and generous, even in conflict. (Would that Congress would realize this.)

COACHING TIPS AND QUESTIONS

If you find yourself in conflict with someone, ask yourself:

- In what ways might I be wrong?
- What's _____'s fondest hope?
- How might I be making that difficult?
- What's it like to be on the receiving end of me?
- How might I be fair and generous toward _____?
- What small or large thing might I do for _____ now?

2-8
SOLVING CIRCLES

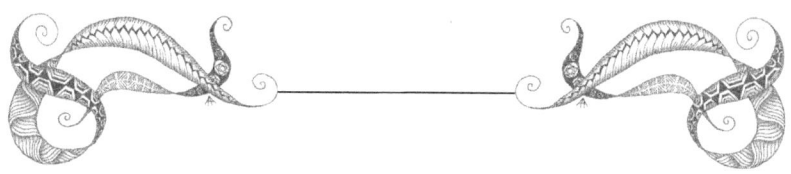

As long as you can stay in the solving circle and accept that you can control only your own behavior, you can negotiate almost anything.
— William Glasser, M.D.

KIRK, AN EFFECTIVE LEADER and sometimes-maverick friend of mine, reflects that two insights provide the foundation for his success. The following are Kirk's words:

1. I have no control over others—I can only control my own behavior (with considerable effort) and influence others (sometimes).

2. Taking the system view, the big picture, a holistic perspective, is the single most effective tool I have to use. The big picture separates what is important from what is a nuisance, allowing me to focus my time and effort on those things that will make a difference.

Kirk notes that he's understood both of these ideas intellectually for a long time. The important change is that now he acts on them consistently. (I suspect the heart of wisdom is acting on what we understand.)

William Glasser combines both of these ideas into a powerful model for conflict resolution that he calls the "solving circle." Using a marital problem as the example, he suggests the partners draw a circle on the floor and sit inside the circle. This is the "solving circle." Inside the circle, there are two individuals (who can't control each other) and the system (the marriage).

The salient question inside the circle is always, "What are we each willing to give (not take) that will help the system (marriage)?" The partners understand that a choice in favor of the marriage may not necessarily be the choice either of them would make for themselves if unmarried.

The solving circle is a useful model in any arena—at work, when departments or co-workers collide, in the world at large, when nations are at odds. Learning to use the solving circle has the potential to save systems as important as the whole earth.

Coaching Tips and Questions

- Whom do you try to control in your life? (When it becomes very clear to us that we can't even control small children, it seems easier to stop trying.)
- How do you react when others try to control you?
- What does your reaction predict will result when you try to control others?
- Where can you use solving circles in your life? (Learn more about them by reading *Choice Theory* by William Glasser.)

2-9

WHAT ARE YOU CARRYING?

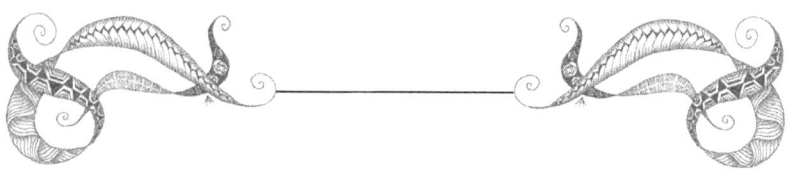

A well-to-do woman with several servants reached a river and needed to cross, but her servants were carrying her many packages and she didn't want them to put the belongings down. Quite self-absorbed, she was verbally abusive and demanding. Finally, two monks came by and one picked her up and carried her across the river, while she continued to berate him and the servants. He put her down on the opposite bank and he and the other monk continued on. After they had walked some time in silence, the second monk blurted out, "I cannot understand it. That woman was rude, arrogant and abusive, and yet you carried her across the river while she cursed at you." The other monk said, "Yes, but I put her down on the river bank hours ago—why are you still carrying her?"

– Zen Story

I'VE HEARD THIS RICH STORY, WITH SLIGHT VARIATION, many times. I asked a number of people what it meant to them. Here's what they said:

- This story helps me leave a lot of things on the river bank—a very energizing thing to do.

- Don't carry around your aggravations!
- It's okay to make a decision to do something for someone even if you don't like them very much—it is YOUR behavior you are responsible for, not theirs.
- A person who carries negative judgments about others pays a high price.

I once saw a video called, simply, *Baggage*. In it there was no talking, just a lovely woman who walked through life, and gradually carried more and more baggage. She started out with a knapsack on her back, and when that got full, she added a Santa-sized bag. Soon she was dragging an unbelievable amount of baggage, and it was literally hard for her to move. The message was vivid.

Now seems like a perfect time to ask ourselves what we're carrying and what we can leave on the riverbank. The good news is that it can be easier than you think.

The most freeing experience of my life was forgiving someone who had hurt me deeply. One day in a blinding flash, I realized how heavy my anger was and how unhappy it kept me. I imagined myself without the anger and the pain. I literally felt light. It was exhilarating! I forgave him on the spot. I was free. The experience was not intellectual—it was about feeling and weight. It happened quickly as I imagined the freedom I would feel when I put my burden down.

Coaching Tips and Questions

- What are you carrying?
  - Old grudges or resentments?
  - Outdated, useless stories?
  - Negative self assessments?
  - Anger?
  - Envy?
  - Too much stuff?
- How would it feel to stop carrying it?
- When will you put it down?

2-10
NO SNIVELING!

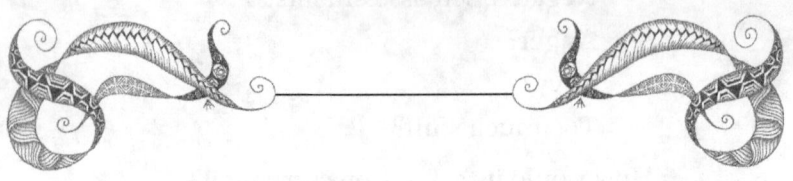

No Sniveling!

– Sign on Senator Ben Nighthorse Campbell's desk

I HEARD RECENTLY THAT 35% OF OUR CONVERSATIONS are complaining. I'm not sure this is accurate, but it got me thinking and listening. In short order I heard people complaining about

- Other people
- The weather
- The food
- The economy
- Aches and pains
- The way things are

For fun, I looked up "complain" and found all these words: protest, criticize, grumble, vent, whine, whinge (my favorite), carp, nitpick, and nag.

There's a lot to be said about complaining. It can be a relief to vent. It can bring people together as they commiserate. It can feel safe.

But even when complaining brings people together and gives them something to agree about (like all the people who can't stand the boss and are happy to share new examples of how horrible she is), complaining is almost always non-productive. Complaining is born of negative energy and grows on itself. Recently, several other people and I were complaining behind the scenes about an educational program we were attending. One woman suddenly said, "Let's not do this anymore. It's not helping." It was a huge relief just to stop because complaining quickly becomes a habit and is contagious.

Coaching Tips and Questions

- Instead of complaining, suggest a solution.
- Instead of complaining, make a request.
- If someone complains to you, ask for a suggested solution or a request.
- If you fall into an "ain't it awful" session, be bold and stop it.
- If you cannot change the source of your complaint, find a way to live with it or work around it. In other words, accept it.

2-11
DO WHAT YOU SAY YOU'LL DO

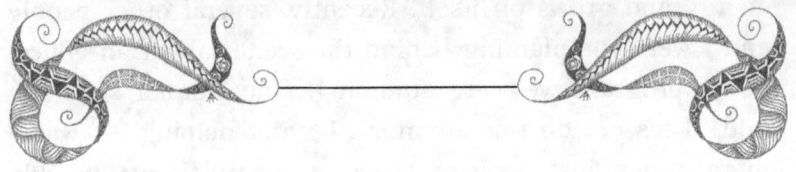

The only possession we own that is worth anything is our word. Unfortunately, many people worry more about scratching their car than keeping their word.

– Douglas D. Chasick

TRUST IS THE BASIS FOR EVERY SUCCESSFUL RELATIONSHIP. This is true when the relationship is between

- Boss and employee
- Service provider and customer
- Husband and wife
- Parent and child
- Friend and friend

The absolutely best way to build trust is to do what you say you'll do. Or tell why not. Every time!

I once worked with the CEO of the Canadian branch of a major U.S. company. People at all levels of the company held the CEO in high esteem. Our assessment showed him to be highly analytical, not a natural people person. "How do you account for your stellar reputation?" I asked him.

He answered simply, "I keep my word."

When we don't pay attention to what we promise, trust suffers. We say, "I'll keep you updated every week," and we don't. We say, "I'll take care of it," and we don't. Or, "I'll call you next week," or "You'll have it by Tuesday," and it doesn't happen. We don't realize that we have broken our word. We have just become untrustworthy.

You can build trust in the following ways:
- Listen to yourself talk and make sure you can do what you say you will do. Then do it.
- If you can't keep your word, acknowledge it. Apologize if you need to. Take responsibility.
- Don't overpromise and underdeliver. It's better to underpromise and overdeliver.

These tips apply equally to communication with your boss, your 5-year-old, your partner, and your best friend.

Chasick also says, "Oh, and by the way, your car is gonna get scratched no matter what you do—that's life!"

Coaching Tips and Questions

- To whom have you failed to keep your word?
- How can you best apologize?
- When, in the next week, will you do it?
- What have you promised that you need to deliver?
- What system do you use to keep track of your promises so that your word is good?
  - If you don't have a system, what have you already thought of that would help?

- When, in the next week, will you institute that system?

2-12

APPRECIATE

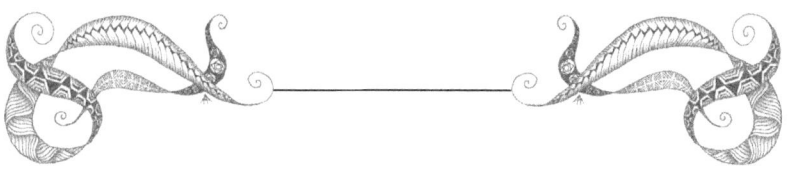

One strong dose of appreciation can turn your perception around 180 degrees.
— Doc Childre and Howard Martin

I'M ALWAYS SEARCHING FOR FOODS THAT
- Taste good
- Are good for me, and
- Are cheap

Peaches fill the bill in late summer. The cost-benefit ratio is superb!

Appreciation is a behavior that meets essentially the same criteria:
- It feels good
- It's good for you
- It's easy

Appreciation involves some blend of thankfulness, admiration, approval, and gratitude. In their breakthrough book, *HeartMath Solution*, Childre and Martin talk about the health benefits of appreciating. Appreciating shifts your heart into a healthy "heart frequency."

We can appreciate just about anything—nature, ideas, art, things, people (even ourselves).

For example, Max, one of my coaching clients, has a teenage daughter, Anna, who was driving him crazy. Her room was a mess and she had to be nagged continually to help with household tasks.

I asked if Max could find anything about Anna to appreciate. He laughed, "She's very funny—always has been." I asked him to look for other things to appreciate in her that week. The next time we talked, Max was relaxed when he talked about Anna.

When he shifted to look for things to appreciate, Max noticed how nice Anna was to her little brother, Joe. Max told Anna he appreciated the way she helped Joe. She said something funny back and they had a good laugh. Later, Max noticed Anna was helping with the dishes.

We can think of "appreciating" as part of a continuum with love and caring. Love is big, wonderful, and sometimes difficult. "Caring for" is often fulfilling and also hard. Appreciating is a tiny shift in your head that is EASY.

In the financial world, something that "appreciates" grows in value. I'm thinking that appreciating appreciates!

Coaching Tips and Questions

- At least five times today and every day for the next week, stop and appreciate something or someone.
- Tell people—including your spouse, children, the clerk at the grocery store, and your boss—what you appreciate about them.

- Develop appreciating into a habit of mind. It may be the single easiest way to improve your life.

2-13
LEARNING FROM A PENGUIN TRAINER

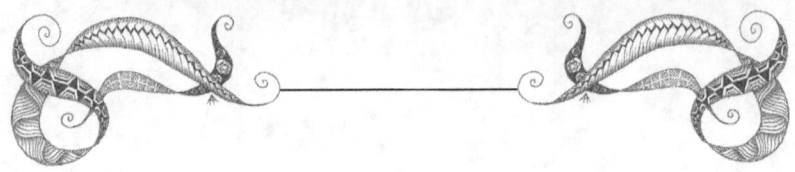

Appreciate that which you want to multiply.
— Bill Veltrop

PSYCHIATRIST DANIEL AMEN TOOK HIS 7-year-old son, whom we'll call Danny, to a marine entertainment park. Freddie the Penguin was their favorite show. Freddie did amazing things: He jumped off a twenty-foot diving board; he bowled with his nose; he counted with his flippers; he even jumped through a hoop of fire. The trainer asked Freddie to get something. Freddie went and got it and brought it right back. Amen thought, "Whoa, I ask my kid to get something for me and he wants to have a twenty minute discussion and then he doesn't want to do it! I know Danny is smarter than Freddie."

After the show, Amen asked the trainer how she got Freddie to do all those neat things. The trainer told him, "Unlike parents, whenever Freddie does anything like what I want him to do, I notice him. I give him a hug and I give him a fish."

The light went on in Amen's head. He realized that whenever Danny did what he wanted him to do, he paid little attention to him, because Amen was a busy guy. However, when Danny didn't do what he wanted him to do, he gave him a lot of attention because he didn't want to raise a bad kid! He was inadvertently teaching his son to be a little monster in order to get Dad's attention.

Amen says, "I collect penguins as a way to remind myself to notice the good things about the people in my life a lot more than the bad things. This has been so helpful for me as well as for many of my patients." (From *Change Your Brain, Change Your Life* by Daniel G. Amen, M.D.)

Coaching Tips and Questions

- Reflect on your responses in the last week toward
    - your kids
    - your parents
    - your partner
    - your co-workers
    - your boss
    - your direct reports
    - your friends
    - your neighbors
- What behaviors did you reward?
- What desirable behavior did you ignore?
- How will you change your responses in the upcoming week?
- Collect a penguin or two to remind yourself of this surprisingly easy behavior.

2-14
PENGUIN TRAINING II

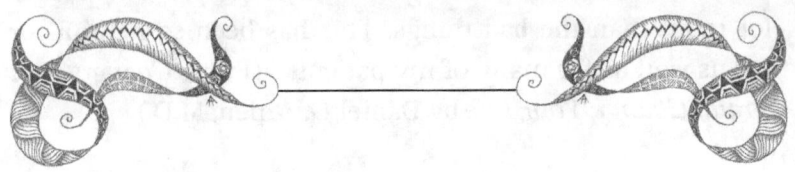

Whenever the penguin does anything like what I want, I notice him...give him a hug and a fish.
— Penguin trainer

WHEN I SHARE DANIEL AMEN'S STORY about the technique used to train penguins (positive reinforcement) people ask some of the following questions:

- Isn't too much praise bad?
- Does this work with people?
- What if the person doesn't like fish?

I did some research and found that this approach works with children, adults, dogs, dolphins, and many other critters. And some refinements make it even more effective.

In answer to questions about too much praise, here's the scoop: Studies have found that children praised for everything they do may begin to view praise as nothing more than "white noise" OR become so dependent on it they expect recognition every time they do something good. Research shows that "intermittent reinforcement" may be more effective. In other words, once children (or penguins or adults) know they will be valued for certain behaviors they will strive to find others that are pleasing, if rewards are not forthcoming every time. This is a relief, because we couldn't possibly be there every time one of our kids or direct reports did something we wanted to see more of!

For applying these ideas in the workplace, I recommend a highly readable book by Douglas and Dwight Allen, *Formula 2+2: The Simple Solution for Successful Coaching*. The Allens help with one of the biggest issues managers have with their staff: communication. Their formula coaches a manager to build a communication style of regular, continuous, positive feedback which makes course corrections much easier.

The 2+2 formula works in families as well.

For penguins, a hug and a fish may be great every time. Research shows that people respond more positively when the recognition

- Acknowledges solid, specific improvement, accomplishment or effort
- Is sincere; phony praise is counterproductive
- Is creative (not a fish or even a hug every time). Comment directly to the person, write a note, tell a third person and ask her to deliver the message, etc.

COACHING TIPS AND QUESTIONS

- What important people in your life will you acknowledge in the next week? Consider family, friends, co-workers, and even your boss.
- If you've already acknowledged a person for one thing, what's another thing (trait, quality, behavior) you appreciate?

- How can you be creative in delivering the acknowledgement?
- How can you do it in a totally sincere way?

2-15

CHOOSE IN EVERY MOMENT

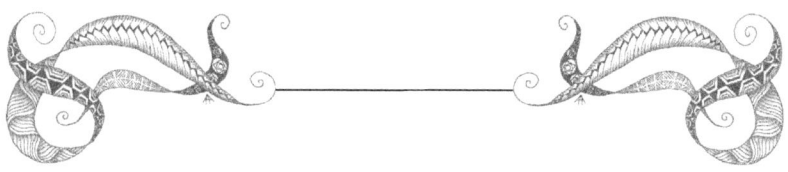

Our lives are a sum total of the choices we have made.

–Wayne Dyer

WITH REALLY BIG THINGS, it's easy to notice we have a choice. What shall I do with the rest of my life? Shall I marry this person? It's harder to realize I'm choosing every moment on little, everyday things. What to do, feel, think, say? How to say it? Shall I be cheerful or grumpy? When I reflect on how many choices I have in a day, I feel both liberated and overwhelmed. Often I'm not even aware of the choices I make. Or it feels like someone else MADE me choose this or that.

Recently I came across something I'd written as an assignment for a class. The assignment was about choosing my way of being. Whew! The goal was to experience what it was like to keep my heart open to another person, choosing to shift the focus off myself enough to see that person fully. Here's the story I wrote:

> Hal and I had been to a long planning meeting, which ended at 6:00 p.m. I'd brought along coupons for a restaurant on the way home, thinking eating out would be better than going home and

cooking. I told Hal my plan. He responded that he'd hoped we could go to Aiello's Pizza place, because he so loved those pizzas and hadn't had one in a long time. I immediately felt the red flag of irritation rise up in me. Aiello's was 20 minutes further away from our house, and we might run into terrible traffic (we had to drive by the baseball stadium and our local team was playing at home). I don't eat cheese, so pizza is out for me, etc.

However, the good news is that I'm recognizing my red flags more quickly, and I really don't like having a warring heart. So, in an instant, I thought of my mother, a huge example for me of an open hearted person, relaxed into her smile, came back to Hal feeling softer toward him, toward my thwarted plan, toward taking him to Aiello's.

I also had a quick insight that I often get attached to my plans and think they're BETTER THAN anyone else's plans (close to home, coupon, no cheese). Hal's request was not that big. I also thought of how I had a choice then, either to go as a martyr, or keep my heart open. I actually had to make the choice right then. Part of me wanted to be martyred. Then I thought of an alternate route that didn't risk game traffic, and off we went.

During the ride, I must admit I was a little pouty, still working on keeping my heart open. Then, when I realized we'd have to park a fair walk from Aiellos, I was annoyed again because we hadn't realized how cold and windy it was and we were underdressed, and Hal walks very slowly. But then I noticed how happy he was and it softened me again. I thought of what a great model he is—that he gets as excited as a little kid over pizza and is willing to walk through the cold to get to it.

I had another moment of annoyance when I studied the menu and saw there really wasn't anything I wanted to eat there. I'm sharing these little moments because I realize how easily I go in and out, teeter on the edge sometimes, feel the irritation rise, and decide whether or not to give in to my warring heart. In the end, Hal LOVED the pizza and expressed his huge appreciation to me. After we got home and I had something to eat that I really liked better than being out, he said to me, "You seem peaceful." And I was.

I loved finding this account in my assignment for so many reasons. It reminded me of Hal, who's no longer with us, and the joy he found in simple things. I was glad to have written this story where I chose well, because I didn't always do that. With Hal most importantly, I was reminded how we truly choose in every moment, and how choosing to have either a peaceful or a warring heart has a huge impact both on my happiness and on the people around me.

Coaching Tips and Questions

- What would be different if you chose to have a heart at peace toward the people in your life?
  - Your family members?
  - Your friends?
  - Your co-workers?

- Your neighbors?
- Other drivers on the road?
- What would it feel like?
- How can you choose to have an open heart toward others more often?
- When will you try it?

2-16

SHIFTS OF HEART

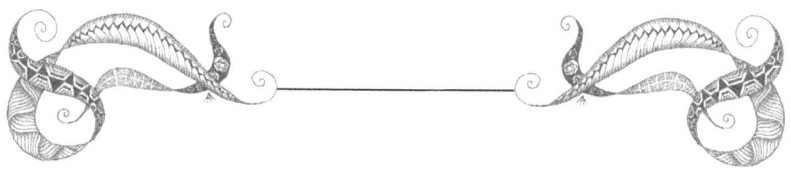

*The most powerful agent of growth and
transformation is a change of heart.*
— John Welwood

A SHIFT OF HEART CHANGES EVERYTHING. When your heart shifts, it changes the way you see the world. Most of us spend effort trying to change our behavior. Welwood's quote gives us a clue to what might bring deeper, more lasting growth and transformation.

EXAMPLES

1. A man boarded a bus with his two unruly children. The children couldn't sit still, nor could they keep their hands off each other. They were loud and many riders were annoyed, even outraged, at the children and their father's seeming acceptance of their bad behavior. Then the father turned to the woman sitting next to him and said sadly, "They don't seem to know what to do since their mother died last week." Imagine how the hearts of those on the bus shifted as they learned the inside story of this man and his children.

2. Robert, a friend of mine, sends a message to all the people he knows every year on his birthday. For years, it was a sad message. Everything went wrong. He and his wife divorced; their special needs child suffered; he lost his job. Robert made attempts to improve things, but nothing helped. It was hard to know how to relate to his black hole. Then one year came a very different birthday message. Robert explained that he had kept a gratitude journal that whole year, writing five things he was grateful for every day. During that year, he had met and was engaged to a wonderful woman; his son was doing well; and he had a new job. He attached his journal, and I read it with delight. As Robert focused on things he was grateful for, they grew and grew and grew. It was as if his heart opened up, and made space for possibility.

3. I was once given this wise counsel about how to soften a tension you're feeling toward someone: Imagine a small thing you could do for this person, then do something even smaller, something the other will not even notice. The value is that this very small kindness opens your own heart, which is what is stuck.

Coaching Tips and Questions

- What are you grateful for right now? (consider keeping a gratitude journal)
- What would love do in your shoes?
- What if you're wrong? (about any situation where you feel you're right)

- What small kindness can you do for someone with whom you feel tension?
- What burden, hope, or dream might that person be carrying?

2-17
ENCOURAGEMENT

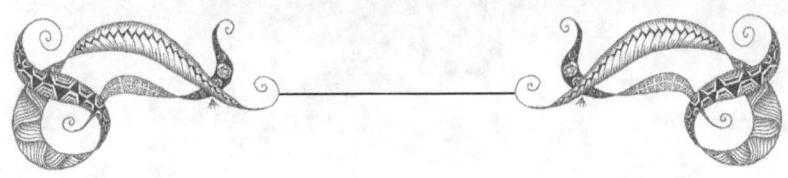

At times our own light goes out and is rekindled by a spark from another person. Each of us has cause to think with deep gratitude of those who have lighted the flame within us.

– Albert Schweitzer

THE SON OF THE FOUNDER of the Bahá'í Faith, 'Abdu'l-Bahá, was once asked to describe the Bahá'í Faith in a single word. Everyone expected him to say, "Unity," or "Peace," because those are right at its core. Instead, his response was "Encouragement."

Here's the dictionary definition of encouragement: to inspire with courage, spirit, or confidence.

When I worked as a therapist, I met many people with personal histories so full of sadness, neglect, or abuse that I wondered how they had survived. I often asked such a person, "Who encouraged you?" In every case, someone had made all the difference: an aunt, a grandma, a neighbor, or a teacher.

Encouragement is to the soul what water is to the body. There are endless sources of potential encouragement, including nature, one's faith, inspiring models, poetry, movies. But on a day-to-day basis, our close relationships offer the biggest opportunity for encouragement—family, friends, co-workers. In fact, research has shown that having an encouraging boss counts more than salary in job satisfaction.

Whenever I reflect on my precious relationship with my late husband, Hal, I am reminded of his ever-present encouragement of me. Hal supported and helped me do everything I wanted to do and be. To be so encouraged was an amazing experience—it gave me roots and wings. Encouragement is related to love, of course, but it feels more tangible. Sometimes Hal's encouragement was just a word or two, as when I'd read him a "Fresh Views" draft and he'd say, "I like it," or "Add a story and it will be great." Or it could be very concrete, such as offering to drive me to upstate New York to attend a week-long meditation retreat. Mutual encouragement was at the heart of our wonderful marriage.

Think of the impact it would have if encouragement were at the center of each of our relationships.

Coaching Tips and Questions

- Who needs your encouragement today at home?
- Who needs your encouragement today at work?
- What stranger might you encourage in some way? (Clerk? Waiter or waitress?)
- What miraculous thing is likely to happen if you encourage others?

2-18

GENEROSITY

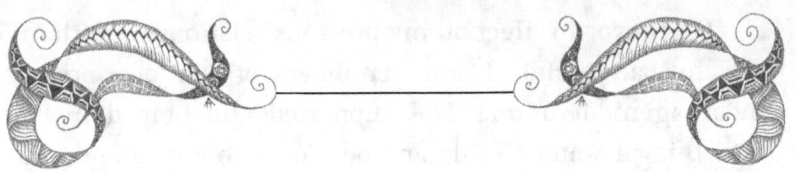

Everyone searches desperately for happiness but the price that we must pay for it is generosity.
– Frederic Back

My favorite dictionary definition of generosity is "freedom from meanness or smallness of mind or character." Perhaps generosity is as much an attitude as an act, holding an open hand instead of a closed fist, an open heart instead of a closed mind.

Thanks to my friends Jan, Sallie, Ann, and Marty for the following thoughts. According to them, generosity

- Is giving of time and energy as much as money
- Is giving beyond what's reasonable or expected
- Can be spontaneous or
- The result of thoughtfulness over time
- Has no strings attached
- Is of the spirit
- Is fun when it's anonymous
- Does good and feels good

The magic of generosity is its circular nature. It is the ultimate win-win-win system. When we give freely, it gladdens our hearts and enriches our souls. Or as the saying goes, "The fragrance remains in the hand that gave the rose."

Generosity seems to have a spiritual effect on the giver, the receiver, and on the universe beyond either. For years, every time I have felt pinched financially, I have given money to a charity. It seems to loosen things up in me and in the universe.

Coaching Tips and Questions

- Who has been generous with you at some point in your life? Think of time, energy, and wisdom as well as material things.

- Where in your life are you naturally generous? How has that worked for you?

- Where in your life would you like to be more generous?

- With whom have you been less than generous? How might things change if you found a way to be more generous toward that person?

2-19

KINDNESS

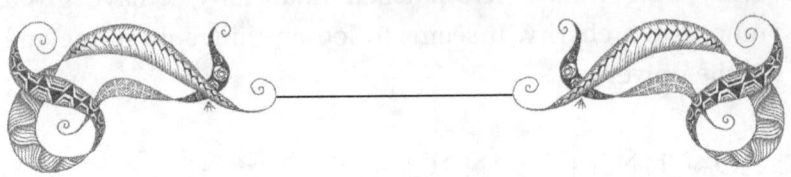

What wisdom can you find that is greater than kindness?

– Jean Jacques Rousseau

HAL AND I OFTEN TOOK A BIKE RIDE after dinner. One day we were nearly home when, starting up from a stopped position, Hal found himself in too high a gear to move forward easily. In slow motion, he fell to the right, hit the sidewalk and broke his hip. A man mowing his lawn stopped and called 911. The paramedics took enormous care not to move the affected leg. A nurse walking by in the emergency room propped Hal's foot in a way that made him more comfortable. Friends fed me and sent Hal cards, fruit, and prayers. A neighbor mowed our lawn. Hal's son installed double handrails to our upstairs. The kindness filled me up and made me want to pass it on.

I am reminded of a retired divorce lawyer I know. As a practicing lawyer, he had a reputation for getting people favorable settlements. Once retired, he reflected on all those divorces and wondered if there was any way he could have helped save marriages instead.

People still call on the lawyer occasionally to help with divorces, so he is engaged in an experiment. He agrees to take a case only if the potential client agrees to his terms, which he promises will "smooth the process." Here are the terms: For one month bend over backwards with kindness toward the spouse you want to divorce.

You can guess the outcome. In almost every case the client falls back in love and decides to stay married.

With kindness, both givers and receivers benefit. Scott Adams said it well, "There's no such thing as a small act of kindness. Every act carries a ripple with no logical end."

Coaching Tips and Questions

- Perform one act of kindness for a stranger this week.
- Perform an extra act of kindness for a loved one this week. (Sometimes we get in the habit of being kinder to strangers than to our loved ones.)
- Perform an act of kindness so small it might go unnoticed. (But how do you feel?)
- Look for ways to do random acts of kindness, which ripple out into the world.
- Check the website of The Random Acts of Kindness Foundation. There you'll find ideas for spreading kindness in your workplace and your community. (www.RandomActsOfKindness.org)

Chapter 3
Be Upbeat

BE UPBEAT

A smile can change the situation of the world.
— Thich Nhat Hanh

Do you know people who are upbeat most of the time? Have you ever wondered how they do it? Most of us have times when we are cheerful, feel good, hopeful, and look forward to the day. But not every day.

I've come to believe it is possible to stay upbeat pretty consistently. But cheerfulness and optimism don't just happen. They have to be cultivated.

You cultivate an upbeat mood with attention to your physical, mental, emotional, and spiritual health. And we all know health in these areas doesn't just happen. It takes time and commitment. For example, what are your answers to the following questions?

- When was the last time you paid attention to how you breathe during the day?
- Can you name your habits, good and bad?
- How do you describe your attitudes towards life, other people, and aging?
- How do you give your mind and body downtime?
- Do you have routines that regenerate both mind and body?
- What percentage of your emotions drains you? What percentage uplifts you?
- Could you benefit from learning to respond rather than react?
- When was the last time you counted your blessings?

It may feel like a difficult dance—balancing all your parts to stay in sync and move forward smiling. A lot of little things help, and that's what this section is about. I want you to live fully and vibrantly, cheerfully working and playing and contributing like crazy, into your dotage.

3-1
BREATHE

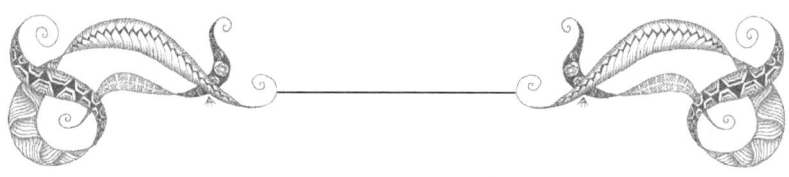

I haven't breathed for 10 days.
— Wonda, New Orleans resident,
10 days after hurricane Katrina

THE ENGLISH LANGUAGE IS FULL OF EXPRESSIONS related to our breathing:

- I'm so busy I can't catch my breath!
- The view is breathtaking!
- Give me some breathing room!

Usually breathing is unconscious—we just do it. We only think about it when there's some problem—we catch a cold and our nose is stuffy or we have a cough. My mother, who is over 90, uses oxygen to help her breathe well. This has increased my awareness of my own breathing.

Breathing is the ultimate systemic activity. With each inhalation, our lungs fill and our heart rate increases to counteract the pressure of the lungs on it. With each exhalation we release, relax, and our heart rate slows down. Everything is affected by our breathing: our blood, muscles, energy, and mood.

Conversely, circumstances inside and outside affect our breathing. When we are hurried, busy, cold, afraid, or angry, our breathing becomes shallow. When we are relaxed and happy, laughing or singing, our breathing is slower, deeper.

If you carefully watch the flow of your breathing, you'll find still points in the midst of the constant change. These are right when you finish breathing in, before you begin to breathe out and at the bottom of the exhalation before the beginning of the next breath.

In their book, *Living in Balance*, Joel and Michelle Levey offer, "The greatest strategy there is for whenever you're feeling particularly frazzled, scattered, and out of balance is simply to return to the awareness of your breathing." It's amazing what conscious breathing can do to improve your mood.

Coaching Tips and Questions

- Become more conscious of your breathing. Several times a day, stop and notice how you're breathing. Take several deep breaths.
- Find the still points in breathing—at the top of the in-breath and the bottom of the out-breath.
- Mimic these very small moments in the rest of your life—stopping for at least a moment when you finish one activity, before beginning the next.
- Read *The Healing Power of the Breath: Simple Techniques to Reduce Stress and Anxiety, Enhance Concentration and Balance Your Emotions* by Richard Brown, M.D. and Patricia Gerbarg, M.D.

3-2
BE HAPPY

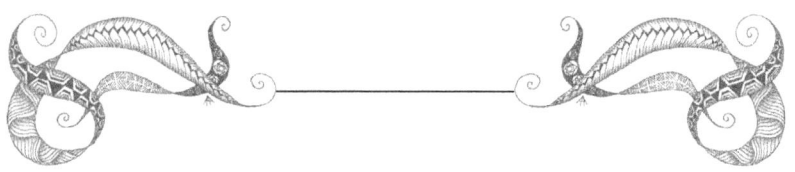

Very little is needed to make a happy life; it is all within yourself in your way of thinking.
— Marcus Aurelius

MOST PEOPLE WANT TO BE HAPPIER, and they have ideas about what would make them happier: a new job, a love partner, more money, moving. The sadness is that most of what we yearn for, thinking it will make us happy, doesn't make us happy after all. Or the happiness is short lived. Then we come up with the next yearning.

Some years ago, the remote South Pacific island of Vanuatu was found to be home to the happiest people on the planet. They are a very poor people. What makes them so happy? I don't really know, but here are my observations about happiness. My guess is that the people in Vanuatu live these things:

> ACCEPT WHAT IS
> People are happiest when they accept what is. I don't recommend that you stop working on making things better. But stop the internal fight with the one that wishes things were different.

Be Grateful

Finding things to be grateful for every day allows even people with very little to be happy. Gratitude literally opens the heart. (Yearning contracts it.)

Be Loving

Loving is the biggest source of happiness. Notice I didn't say being loved, although that's terrific. Nevertheless, the act of loving fills us up! The object of the love can be a person or people, a cause, or even your work. So find a person or a cause to pour your heart into, regardless of what comes back to you.

Strive to love well. If you don't have a person to love close at hand, volunteer somewhere and find someone: A baby in a neonatal unit who needs to be held, a child who needs a big brother or sister or grandparent. Or dedicate yourself to a cause you believe in deeply—the environment, a particular illness, human trafficking, your religion, whatever moves you, and give it all you've got.

When clients tell me they want to find a life partner, my advice is to work on acceptance, gratitude, and love. A sad or desperate person is not attractive. A person who has found ways to be happy in his or her current life already has love flowing out and is very attractive.

A couple of years ago I had cancer. People have asked me how I got through that time so easily. These three things helped me see that illness as an interesting, even blessed, chapter in my life. After the initial shock, I accepted that even though I'd never expected to have cancer, I did. There were a couple of days after each chemotherapy treatment when I felt lousy, so I slept and read books on those days.

The rest of the time, I went about my life as usual. I lost my hair, so I got cute head coverings. I was grateful to forgo the task of washing and caring for my hair. I was amazed and grateful for all the support I received. And maybe because cancer is a brush with death, I was able to see and love the people in my life more fully. I paid better attention. And I stayed happy through the whole experience, which probably helped me heal.

For a lasting happiness, try these three steps:
1. Accept what is
2. Be grateful
3. Love with all your heart

Coaching Tips and Questions

- What are you fighting in your life that you could just accept? When will you do it?
- What are you grateful for right now?
- Try making a list of five things you're grateful for every day.
- Who or what do you really care about?
  - How can you love that person or that cause more fully?
  - How can you express that love?
- If you can't think of anyone or anything, how can you find someone or something to love? Happiness without this movement of the heart tends not to last.

3-3
DON'T SEEK BALANCE

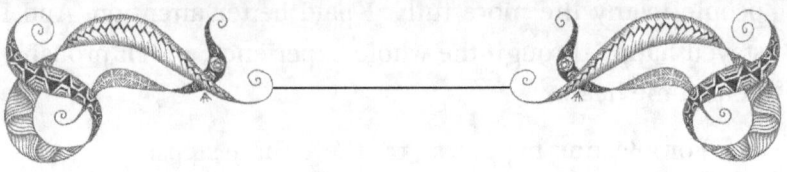

Do what brings you joy.

– David Burnett

AS A COACH, I OFTEN HEAR PEOPLE SAY, "I need more balance in my life." The image of making a mobile as a child at summer camp pops into my mind. We made mobiles by hanging shells and bits of beach debris on driftwood twigs. It was fun and challenging to create a balanced mobile. Even when I got the mobile perfect, a breeze could undo the balance. A small tweak could bring it back.

What does balance mean to you?
- An equal amount of work and play?
- Structured and unstructured time?
- Some match of things you HAVE to do and things you WANT to do?

Maybe we complicate it all too much.

David Burnett suggests a simpler approach, where joy is the leverage point in the system that is us:

> Do what brings you joy, and systematically take care of things that interfere with joy. The result will be more balance as well as more joy!

Burnett's approach leads to a freeing practice. When I keep my focus on joy, I do more of the following:

- Play with my kitty
- Say "No" to things I don't really want to do
- Participate in relationships differently
- Decide not to do some things
- Laugh more
- Decide to do some things badly (or not perfectly)
- Slow down and live more in the present

Coaching Tips and Questions

- What gives you joy? Make a list of at least 10 things.
- What interferes with your having what gives you joy? Make a list of at least 5 things.
- How can you start systematically taking care of the things that interfere with joy?
- When will you start?

3-4
WHAT'S RIGHT?

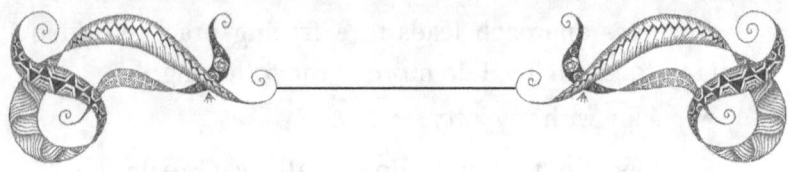

Instead of asking, "What's Wrong?" ask, "What's Right?"

– Kurt Wright

WHILE ON A MUCH-ANTICIPATED VACATION at Martinak State Park in Maryland, Hal got sick. We first thought he had twisted his hip paddling our new kayak on its maiden voyage. By the second night, however, I grew concerned that Hal's sore hip was really a flare-up of a chronic infection in his back that is monitored regularly by folks at the Mayo Clinic. Worrying about this kept me awake, which I realized was not going to help. I had been reading Kurt Wright's book, *Breaking the Rules, Removing the Obstacles to Effortless High Performance*. He suggests focusing on what is right at any given moment, instead of focusing on what is wrong. I decided to try it. I laid there and created a list in my head:

- Hal was sleeping peacefully beside me.
- Our tent was dry in spite of having had a huge storm.
- The inflatable mattress was amazingly comfortable.

- We had had a lovely day at the ocean and ate delicious crab cakes.
- We had wonderful doctors we could call in the morning.
- We had a thermometer with us and could take Hal's temperature.
- We had had a fun time kayaking on Watts Creek. It was beautiful and we were gaining paddling skill. (The first time we kayaked, we went in circles a lot and accidentally hit each other with the paddles.)

I fell asleep picturing us skimming along in our kayak on a beautiful river. In the morning, Hal had a temperature. We called the doctor. In a short time, we were on our way home. Before you knew it, we were at the Mayo Clinic and Hal was being cared for in the Clinic's incomparable way. All the way, I kept track of what was right. The Mayo Clinic itself offers an amazing opportunity to study what's right, but that's another story.

Hal was quickly better, and we shared years of kayaking happily, with more and more skill, on our own Ohio River.

This experience was not just a feel-good exercise. The shift from focusing on "What's Wrong?" to "What's Right?" was profound for me. I could easily have become overwhelmed by anxiety and fear. Focusing on what was right both relaxed and energized me, so I could do what was needed. Wright says "What's Right?" questions help us access an intuitive part of the brain and release creative energy.

Coaching Tips and Questions

Wright offers a five-question framework for using "What's Right?" questions to help individuals or teams solve problems. Try them by asking:

- What's RIGHT? Or What's working?
- What makes it RIGHT? Or Why does it work?
- What would be ideally RIGHT? Or What would work ideally?
- What's not yet quite RIGHT?
- What resources can I find to make it RIGHT?

3-5

HELPING THINGS GO RIGHT

You can either focus on what's wrong or help things go right.
— Arbinger Institute concept

A COUPLE OF YEARS AGO, MY DAUGHTER, LISA, flew from Sacramento to Washington D.C. and I met her there from Pittsburgh so we could attend a conference together. We had a wonderful time, attending workshops together and separately, walking hand-in-hand down Connecticut Avenue, having long, slow, delicious meals, with the rare time to chat to our heart's content and be silent too. On our last night together in the hotel room we watched a movie, and went to bed early.

Little did we know our room was next to a big ballroom, where our conference presenters were having a celebration. The noise level began to rise. I called the front desk around 10:30 to complain and ask what could be done. They said they'd send someone up to ask the group to be quieter. Sure. It got louder and louder.

Finally, Lisa picked up the phone. I braced myself. She has always been a light sleeper and sleep disturbance annoys her. I will never forget what happened next. In the nicest voice, she asked to speak to the manager on duty. A very short time later, the manager called. Lisa explained that nothing was wrong. It was just that people were having a big party next door and she and her mother needed to sleep. She suggested that they give us a different room for the night and allow us to leave all of our things in the first room since we were in our nighties, etc.

The manager said they were very full, but he'd see what he could do. Ten minutes later, he called and invited us to meet him at a room on the other side of the hotel. We put hotel robes on over our nighties and trekked through the halls at midnight. Halfway there we almost fell down giggling, as we realized we'd have to make the trip back in the morning, still in our nighties. Lisa had helped things go right.

It is so easy and natural to focus on what's wrong, to dwell on it, to get worked up about it. The trouble is that when I'm focused on what's wrong, I'm usually in a blaming mood. The problem is always outside of me, outside my control. The idea of helping things go right is very different. It calls me to examine myself, the humanity of the situation, and/or the other person involved. To examine how I might even be contributing to what's wrong. It is useful to ask oneself, "Is what I'm about to say going to help or hurt the situation?" And if the answer is "hurt," consider not saying it.

Of course, helping things go right sometimes means speaking up and saying what is hard. I once served on a committee to remodel and redecorate a large lounge used by drug and alcohol patients. I was there to represent the patients' interests with the architects. I had already voiced concerns about the practicality of their beautiful proposals. They seemed deaf to me. As final decision time came, I realized that of course, the architects wanted the lounge to be beautiful, but if I didn't speak up loud and clear, we would soon have a beautiful, non-functional lounge for our patients. I spoke clearly and forcefully about what worried me. They heard. Working together creatively, the end results were both beautiful and functional.

Coaching Tips and Questions

Reflect on the happenings in your life over the past two weeks.

- Where in your life are you focused on what's wrong?
- How might you be contributing to what's wrong?
  - Blaming?
  - Missing the humanity in the person or situation?
  - Acting out old scripts?
- What would be different if you focused on helping things go right?

3-6
STOPPING AND STARTING

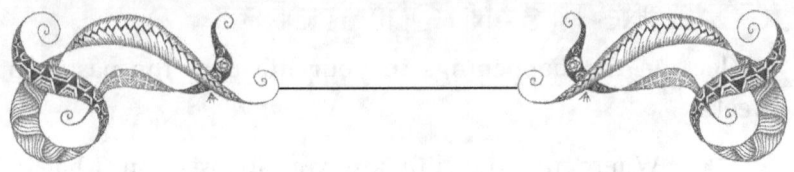

In the name of God, stop a moment, cease your work, look around you.

– Leo Tolstoy

I YEARN TO BE A BETTER PROCRASTINATOR. One of my goals is to stop more. Once I get going, it is hard for me to stop. I just keep moving. If there are things calling to be done, I do them until I'm ready to drop. I have to practically sit on myself to meditate. And yet, when I do, it makes me so happy. When I stop to visit with a friend, draw, or take pictures, I am infinitely happier than I was before. But the pull to do what's on my list, to take care of everything in my environment (family member, cat, plants, outside birds, clothes, mail, and stuff) is very strong.

One of the dangers of constant busyness without stopping is that I may get on some path and keep moving, even when the path doesn't go where I want to go.

One reason I think coaching works is that it requires people to stop and reflect on what they're doing and feeling, where they're going. When I am coached, it's as if I come back to myself, rest my weary bones, and in the process get perspective, energy, and room for new ideas.

I know people who are just the opposite from me. They have trouble getting started. Or they start but quit easily. These people tend to be mad at themselves a lot. They want to do things but don't know how to start. When they do get started, they are easily discouraged when difficulties arise, or they get overwhelmed and stop.

It's hard to find the right balance of activity. Our priorities and relationships suffer when we don't stop—or if we don't start. Without balance, it's hard to live our values—things like kindness, health, and honesty. So what's the middle ground? And how do we get there? I don't really know the answer, but this year I'm going to try a different approach. Instead of trying to force myself into new habits, I commit to two things:

1. Focus on the relationships in my life. Each day I will reflect on how well I'm living the relationships I care about.
2. Focus on the values I hold dear. Each day I will reflect on how well I'm living my values.

I hope that by putting the focus on what really matters to me—people and values—I'll stop more. When I stop more, I am more cheerful!

Coaching Tips and Questions

- Are you someone who has trouble stopping or has trouble starting? Maybe a first step is to become aware of your own tendencies. Maybe you can be both—in different areas of your life.
- What trouble does your not stopping/starting cause the people in your life?
- How does your not stopping/starting keep you from living your values?

- Try this: For a full day, focus on helping your relationships with important people in your life go well. Notice if you're stopping or starting changes.

- On another day, focus on living your values all day. See how that affects your stopping and starting.

- Does doing the thing that's hard for you—stopping or starting—affect your cheerfulness?

3-7
EMOTIONS

The little emotions are the great captains of our lives and we obey them without realizing it.
— Vincent Van Gogh, 1889

EMOTIONS ARE WITH US EVERY MINUTE of every day. Stop for a moment right now and ask yourself what emotion you're feeling. If you have trouble naming the emotion, here's an exercise that might help: Write for five minutes non-stop, listing every emotion you can think of. My friend Sharon Lippincott, author of *The Heart and Craft of Lifestory Writing*, recently suggested this exercise on her blog.

"Five minutes, now that's something I can do," Sharon said. And in five minutes she had dumped out a list of 64 emotions. "I was pumped, stoked, thrilled, and energized. I was also hooked," she said. Later her list grew to hundreds.

Always interested in emotions, I decided to try my hand. "Anxiety, joy, exhilaration, love," I wrote. Once you start, you can't stop thinking about emotions—their subtleties, the tangle of emotions, thoughts, and actions. What you feel and how you respond. I woke up the next morning ready to write fresh, emotional words: invigorated, irritated, grateful ....

The trouble with emotions is that they seem to have a life of their own. You can ignore them, but they don't always go away. The evolution of the field of emotional intelligence, popularized by Daniel Goleman, makes it clear that learning to identify and manage one's emotions is among the most important skills of a successful person. Goleman talks about the basic families of emotion: anger, sadness, fear, enjoyment, love, surprise, disgust, and shame. Other emotions may be seen as extended family members.

I recently met a delightful little boy named William. He is in the third grade and has severe autism. This means that he doesn't easily pick up social cues from others or know what is appropriate. But he's learning fast. William told me the thing that helps him most is his "emotion meter," which is a little strip of paper he carries in his pocket with the numbers 1 to 5 on it. "Whenever I feel an emotion coming into my body," he says, "I pull this out and figure out where I am from 1 to 5, so I'll know how to act." William explained how he interprets his scale:

- If it's a 1, like maybe a tag rubbing on my neck, I'm just irritated. So instead of tearing off my clothes and screaming, I just ignore it.
- If it's a 2, I'm frustrated, and instead of calling 911, I walk away.
- If it's a 3, I'm angry and deep breaths really help.
- If it's a 4, I'm furious and need a yellow break card, so I can go out of the room and do wall pushups.
- If it's a 5, I'm enraged and use my yellow break card to leave the situation, do wall pushups, and get a big drink of water.

William is learning to identify and manage his emotions. We can all learn from him. He's learning that some emotions can be ignored safely while others need attention and resolution.

Jonatan Martensson said, "Feelings are much like waves, we can't stop them from coming, but we can choose which one to surf."

Coaching Tips and Questions

- See how many emotions you can list in five minutes.
- Follow William's tip and pay attention to when an emotion is coming into your body. See if you can name it.
- Ask yourself where this emotion is on your emotion meter.
- Ask yourself if this is an emotion you want to surf or not.
- Imagine capturing your emotion in a piece of art. What color would it be? What would you use to make it? If your painting, sculpture, drawing, or some other art expression feels clear, make it.

3-8
SILENCE

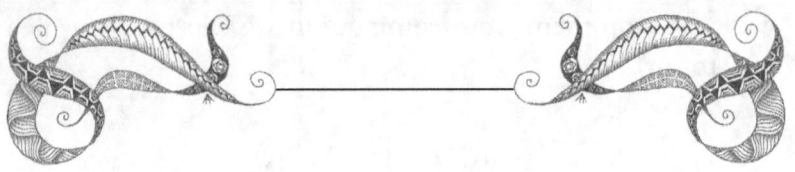

He had occasional flashes of silence that made his conversation delightful.
— Sydney Smith

WHEN I FIRST READ SMITH'S QUOTE above, I chuckled in recognition. I love being with people who are comfortable with silence. We talk and then we fall silent, and it is nice. This kind of relationship provides comfortable companionship.

A couple of my friends say they avoid silence. It seems almost scary. They enjoy the comfort of sound—TV or music, even if they aren't paying any attention to it.

Pondering silence took me back to several memorable experiences of silence.

- I once attended a Quaker gathering where the focus was a topic of great interest. There were only two rules: 1) Each person had to speak once before any person could speak a second time; and 2) after each speaker, there were two minutes of silence. The effect was profound. Imagine how this format would change business meetings!

- Miss Fuller, my childhood piano teacher, once chided me for speeding through a piece. "Without the rests, the silences, there is no music," she said.

- I co-teach a 15-week teleclass for coaches. When the group, usually 6-9 people, gets really comfortable with each other, there are often long, thoughtful silences in response to a question. When someone speaks, it is sometimes profound, as if the silence allowed the individual to go deep for the answer.

It was said of a distinguished general, "He can hold his tongue in 10 languages."

Coaching Tips and Questions

- Practice growing the silence in your life. In the next week, turn off all music, radio, and TV for just a few minutes. What do you become aware of?

- For two nights in the next week, try being in total silence for 10 minutes before you go to sleep. How do you sleep?

- If you are in charge of a meeting, start with 30 seconds of silence to allow attendees to move fully from whatever they were just doing to the meeting. What difference does this make?

- The next time someone asks you a tough question, say, "Let me think about that for a minute." Then be silent awhile before you answer. How does the quality of your answer change?

3-9
Expect Surprises

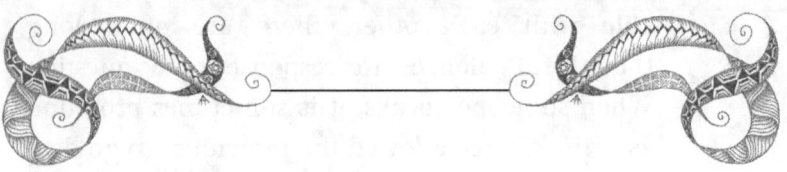

History is merely a list of surprises. It can only prepare us to be surprised yet again.
— Kurt Vonnegut, Jr.

My cat Bonkers is 11 years old and pretty set in his ways. According to the cat calculator, he's the equivalent of 61 human years old. Imagine my surprise last night when this highly predictable creature dared to step on a fluffy bathroom rug that he has pointedly avoided for over two years. Before I got this fluffy rug, Bonkers always visited me when I was taking a bath. He loved to sit and watch me, then stand with front paws on the tub and dip his toe in, sometimes talking to me in a gurgling voice. As much as I loved the new rug, Bonkers didn't. He'd come to its edge, look up at me, and leave. Then last night I suddenly heard that old familiar voice and looked over to see him sitting on and kneading the fluffy rug. Soon he stood tall and dipped his toe in the water, as if two scared years had not passed.

I love these surprises in relationships with Bonkers, friends, clients, family, and even strangers. Toward the end of his life, my husband Hal got sweeter and sweeter. He had the ability to be curmudgeonly, so this was a delightful surprise.

Last week a client told me, happily, that she'd called her father, from whom she'd been estranged for several years. They had a lovely conversation. I asked her how she did it. "I surprised myself," she said. "I was sitting here thinking about my dad, and how funny he could be. Suddenly I missed him, so I picked up the phone. All those petty things didn't even matter. What was even more surprising was how happy he seemed to hear from me."

Sometimes even when something is expected, it surprises. For example, how do all the forsythia decide on the same day to burst into brilliant yellow bloom?

Sometimes surprises are huge, impacting thousands of people. For example, people close to the situation had predicted the Berlin Wall would stand for 50 or 100 more years. And yet, in 1989, it was dismantled almost overnight, leading to the 1990 reunification of Germany after 28 years of separation.

Sometimes surprises are shocking, like when two bombs went off at the Boston marathon. Some people were killed and many were injured.

Sometimes good surprises come out of bad. I was certainly surprised to be diagnosed with endometrial cancer and the need to go through life-saving treatment. I continue to be amazed at the love and support I've received from countless family and friends as I've bounced back.

Sometimes surprises are funny. Last week when entering a car wash, I had trouble getting my car into neutral. I rolled down the window to tell the guy just as he aimed his pre-wash spray in my face. He was horrified, but I just laughed and laughed.

For me the takeaway about surprises is this: Be open to surprises—look for them. The negative ones have a way of hitting us on the head so we won't miss them. But if we get jaded or cynical, we can easily miss the good ones. Being open to—even expecting—surprises is an upbeat way to live. And experiencing and appreciating the good surprises can build resilience for the bad ones.

Coaching Tips and Questions

- What recent surprise delighted you?
- Are you open to, even expecting, surprises?
- How do you use the good surprises to help you cope with the bad ones?
- Reflect on one or more negative surprises you experienced in life. What good came out of them?

3-10
EFFORTLESSNESS

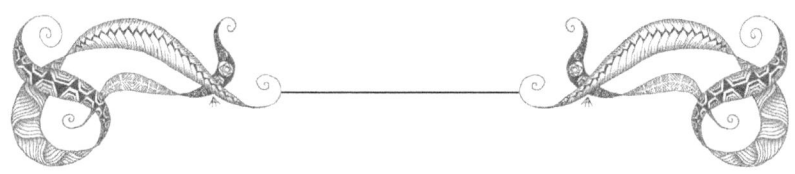

Relax your way into the pose. If you muscle your way into it, you'll hurt yourself.
— Ruth Rittenhouse, yoga teacher

WHEN I HAVE LOTS TO DO, I often get weary IN ADVANCE!

There IS another way, and sometimes I'm able to do it. I think of this "other way" as EFFORTLESSNESS. It involves shifts in both doing and thinking. Here are some I can identify:

SHIFTS IN DOING
- Do what's easy, what you're good at. When you run into hard stuff, get someone to do it with you. Sing, joke, and take breaks.
- Make a list of what you want to accomplish, but don't look at it again. Just do what you feel to do. The list will get you focused, but you're not a slave to it.
- Chunk a task into small pieces. For example, I clean up an impossible basement in 30 minute bursts.

- Follow your energy. STOP when you're tired, even if it feels like you MUST keep going. Resting for 10 to 30 minutes will refresh you.
- If you want to do something that takes huge, sustained effort, plan downtime for recovery afterward.

SHIFTS IN THINKING
- Recognize that a great deal of what is worthwhile is easy and fun, rather than saying to yourself, "Everything worthwhile is hard."
- Be in discovery mode rather than drudgery mode. Instead of "pre-paving" for effort and exhaustion, "pre-pave" for ease and adventure.
- When you find yourself thinking negatively, (worried, fearful, mad, bored, or frustrated) do something immediately to switch the direction of your mood. Smile, laugh, think of something or someone funny, think of something you want to do, think of someone you love—anything to reverse the direction of your energy. Do this many times a day if needed.
- Be open to the outcome—things might turn out differently (even better!) than you'd imagined.

It's ironic to me that just as relaxing my mind and muscles allows me to get into amazing yoga poses, when I'm in effortless mode, I accomplish more and am happier to boot.

Coaching Tips and Questions

- Think of one area of your life that feels burdensome.
- Imagine that it could be effortless.
- Read the bullets under "Shifts in Doing" above and do one or more of them.
- Read the bullets under "Shifts in Thinking" above and do one or more of them.

3-11

Be Early

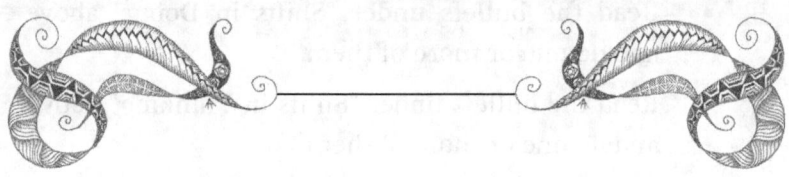

The early bird catches the worm.

– Adage

Have you ever noticed that people tend to be consistently early, consistently on-time, or consistently late? I've known couples where this is a major issue in the relationship until either they work out a conscious compromise or one adopts the other's style.

I've always been the right-on-time type myself. Somehow, I feel good about my ability to calculate just what I can get done before leaving, just how much time it will take me to get somewhere, and as I walk in at 1:59 for the 2:00 meeting, I smile, "Yes!"

Recently, I accidentally got to a meeting early. A phone appointment was cancelled, and I simply left when I was ready, arriving at the meeting sixteen minutes early. To my amazement, there were already several people there.

This was like visiting a new country—I didn't know what early people do. They have relaxed conversations, walk around, get settled, go to the restroom, talk on their cell phones BEFORE the meeting. I was astonished and delighted.

The next day, I purposely added fifteen minutes to what would have been my usual requirement to get to an appointment on time. And good thing. Because there was construction blocking the parking area, and I had to find a parking spot and walk two blocks, and I was only four minutes early. It seemed like this message was getting stronger.

I began paying attention to the energy of people with these various styles. The early birds are definitely more relaxed. The on-timers are a little tense but proud of themselves. The latecomers often try to be invisible, yet arrive surrounded by a cloud of tension from the rush.

You may think of being early as a waste of time. Things never start on time, so why get there early just to wait. Try having something with you so you can be productive while you wait, or use the waiting time to be thoughtful. Last week I was early to an appointment with someone who was late. I had thirty glorious minutes to organize my next couple of weeks.

Sometimes situations don't allow you to be early. This fast-paced world often sets it up so you have to leave one meeting early just to be late at the next. Many times, however, being early may require only a slight shift in your thinking. I'm not committed to BECOMING an early person, but I think I'll try it more often. I challenge you to experiment with this for two weeks. See what happens to your energy and/or tension.

COACHING TIPS AND QUESTIONS

- Be early to meetings and appointments.
- For two weeks, make the shift in your thinking and your behavior required to be early to things.

- Decide ahead of time when you need to leave your house or work space to get to the meeting or appointment early. Then do it.
- Notice any differences you experience inside yourself and as a response from others because of your being early.
- Decide consciously whether to be an early, on time, or late person going forward.

3-12

PATIENCE

A handful of patience is worth more than a bushel of brains.
— Dutch Proverb

MY PATIENCE PAID OFF. Since he was a kitty, Bonkers, my 12-year-old cat, has insisted on drinking water ONLY from his dad's big glass on the kitchen table. It was a little embarrassing, but you don't get far disagreeing with Bonkers. However, as Bonkers has gotten older, that leap to the tabletop has gotten harder. Though I'd failed many times before, I decided to see if he would drink water from a glass on the floor. I put a fresh glass near his food every day. It only took six weeks before he tried it. And now he drinks all his water from there. I just had to be patient.

Instead of trying to define patience, let me share some of its many benefits.

1. Patience makes you and the people around you happy and peaceful. Compare the way it feels to BE or BE WITH a patient driver and an impatient driver.

2. Patience brings acceptance—calling us to the present moment, helping us respond instead of react to bad news, loss, or difficulties.

3. Patience can bring healing. My husband Hal became legally blind. He was told there was nothing to be done about cone dystrophy. He didn't believe it. He knew a lot about the brain and decided to try his own method to restore sight. He theorized that if he could produce more stem cells, he would recruit them to his retina and see again. He practiced every single day for more than two years with no sign of change. One day at the grocery store, well into the third year, he said, "Does that aisle sign say RICE?" It DID. I wept. His doctors called it a miracle, which it truly was. Hal created this miracle, from perseverance and faith, which are components of patience.

4. Patience can solve problems, as it did with Bonkers' water. Maybe this is just developing a friendlier relationship with time. Sleeping on something and finding the solution right there in the morning. Continuing to try a potential solution even when the results are slow to come.

Patience is not all passive. Someone even called patience "concentrated strength." It often takes more effort to be patient than to take many actions!

In this age of instant everything, how can we grow our patience and teach it to our children? Here are some ideas. I hope you'll have others.

- Notice whenever you feel the creep of impatience coming on. Identify your own clues: biting your lip, rising anger, or a tense stomach.
- Stop. Ask yourself to slow down. Take time to think, and then respond instead of reacting.

- Tune in fully to others. Listen deeply. Get fascinated with others and what they have to say.
- Consider taking yoga or meditation classes. These are now being taught in prisons, in colleges, and to small children. The positive experiences are making for more patience and peace in peoples' lives.

> *Patience is a kind of love. A love that is its own explanation in bewildered circumstance. It is an old, old woman placing a wrinkled-parchment hand against the cheek of a reckless child. Because her heart is too wise to make room for reproach. Too full to find place for offense.*
>
> – Pavithra Mehta

Coaching Tips and Questions

- Which of the four benefits of patience listed above do you need to be happier, to accept something, to heal, to solve problems?
- With whom or in what situations could you use more patience?
- How willing are you to commit to cultivating more patience (on a scale from 1 to 10)?
- Which of the four steps above are you willing to try?
- When will you start?

3-13

Fun

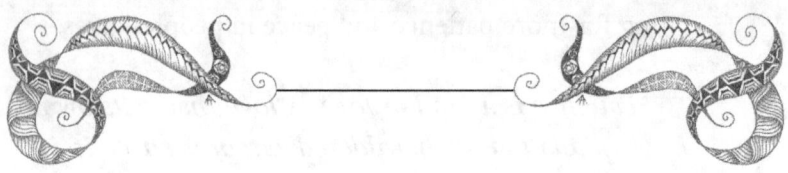

While most of us do not feel as driven by fun as we are by power, freedom or belonging, I believe it is as much a basic need as any other.
— William Glasser, M.D.

My 15-year-old granddaughter, Ruthie, was visiting from California. "Shall I write about how important it is to take a vacation?" I asked her. "No," she answered quickly. "Write about fun." (I think she suggested this because we're having a lot of it!)

As soon as Ruthie suggested "fun" as the topic, I was reminded of the above quote from Glasser, a well-known psychiatrist. I went back to his book, *Reality Therapy,* where Glasser makes a strong and fascinating case for fun. He says that we actually NEED fun to learn.

Through fun, we learn not only what our needs are but also how to get those needs met. Think of puppies or kittens playing, obviously having fun. Glasser notes that most primates stop playing as they grow to adulthood because they have learned all they need to know. Humans, however, are more complex and must learn all their lives. So if we learn through fun, we need to have fun throughout our entire lives.

Stop right now and evaluate: What is fun for you? Are you having fun in your life?

Seeing the connection of fun to learning may point to the biggest problem in our education system. Assuming learning is a serious business, the system squeezes the fun out! Think back to your own favorite teachers. I'll bet they had some way of infusing lightness and fun into the learning.

Glasser suggests that many long-term relationships grow stale and unsatisfying because fun is neglected, taken for granted, or not felt as much needed by one of the partners as the other. Think of your partner, or someone you love. Do you know what fun is for them? Do you support fun in their lives?

Conversation with friends Sallie and Dell added the following perspectives on fun:

- Fun is an attitude and a choice.
- Fun is different for different people. For example, some people like golf, others hate it; some prefer competitive sports, others cooperative, etc.
- Anticipating fun is also fun.
- Some fun is hard work—like preparing for a big hike or a triathlon. The payoff is in the endorphins that are generated, the fitness that results, the camaraderie, and the empowerment.
- The unexpected is often fun.
- Doing things with people we enjoy makes anything fun.
- When something resonates and we laugh or giggle together, there is a sense of connection.
- Work can and should be fun.

Ruthie and I experienced how work can be fun when doing it together. She and I steam-cleaned and put a new finish on my hardwood floors. It was hard work, but we giggled, moved quickly, and accomplished the task in 1/5 of the time it takes me to do it alone. We felt cheerful both while we were working and later, because the floors are now so beautiful!

If fun is so important, we need to pay more attention to it, noticing when we are making the choice for fun and when we are making the choice against fun.

Coaching Tips and Questions

- What is fun for you?
- How could you have more fun in your life?
- When you are doing a difficult task, how can you make it fun?
- What is fun for your partner/dear one?
- How can you support that?
- What can you do WITH someone that will make it more fun?
- How can you infuse fun into your work?
- Choose two of the above and commit to doing them within a week.

3-14

TAKE A BREAK

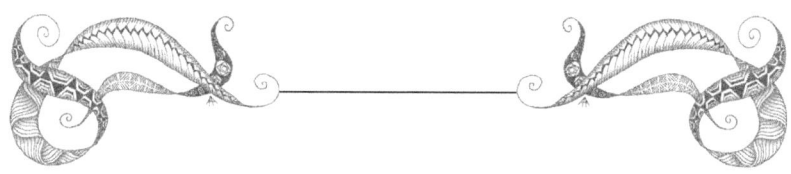

A vacation is what you take when you can no longer take what you've been taking.
— Earl Wilson

HAVE YOU TAKEN A VACATION IN THE LAST YEAR? If not, do you have one planned? The best practice is to book your next vacation the minute you get home from one. It lets you plan, get input from others, fantasize, and savor the idea of getting away.

WHY YOU NEED A BREAK

In order to be creative and productive over time, you need to interrupt all the systems in your life periodically. This means your body needs a change of pace, and you need a change of scenery, a break in your usual rhythm, and your daily routines. Ironically, you need a change of perspective to come back to yourself.

A vacation helps you remember that you, your family, and your work are small, important parts of something bigger; there is a whole, interesting world out there. Often even a short break brings clarity to some issue you've been struggling with, without your working on it consciously. It's as if your subconscious mind needs your conscious mind to stop chattering so it can see its way to clarity.

This time-out-from-the-usual is also physically restorative. Hopefully, a break allows you to rest, often making up for a lack of sleep.

Sometimes it's impossible to take a long break. Here's the good news: Short breaks can work miracles. Here are some ideas for short breaks:

- Spend one or two nights at a B&B a short distance from home. Don't plan much.
- Find a retreat house near your home and go by yourself for a couple of days.
- Meet a friend from another city at a motel or B&B midway between your homes.
- Rent a cabin at a state park near you for a couple of days.
- Ride the train to another city. Take in a ballgame or a show, stay overnight or not, and head back home.
- Find a festival or a summer theater less than two hours away. Spend the night near there.
- Check out last-minute plane or cruise sales on the Internet, or call a travel agent and ask about these. Unfilled plane, ship, and hotel slots are often 50 to 75% off. The companies are happy to get something instead of nothing for an available spot.
- Leave your kids with a relative or friend and go somewhere you'd enjoy just overnight. Return the favor for the friend.

If you truly can't get away, for whatever reason, there are still ways you can take a break that interrupts your systems. Change your routine drastically. You'll be amazed how doing this refreshes you and increases your creativity. Try one of these or make up your own:

- Outside of required reading at work or school, don't read anything at all for a week. This idea, called reading deprivation, is from Julia Cameron's book, *The Artist's Way*. I once did this, found it very difficult, but began dancing all over the house before the week was out!
- Take a break from the news for a full week. Don't watch TV news or listen to radio news, or read the newspaper. I promise you, nothing much will change.
- Take a break from TV for a week. Put tape over the power on/off button on the remote.
- Change the radio station settings on your car radio. Listen to something totally new.

Without breaks, the fast lives many people lead are unsustainable. For your physical, mental, emotional, and spiritual health, become skilled at taking regular breaks. You'll be glad you did.

Coaching Tips and Questions

- If you don't have a break planned, what can you start planning right now?
- If you do have a break planned, enjoy. What can you plan for your next break?

- Commit to three ways to interrupt your routine in the next week.

3-15
GRATITUDE

Gratitude is not only the greatest of virtues but the parent of all others.
— Cicero

THANKSGIVING MAY COME ONCE A YEAR, but gratitude is such a powerful phenomenon it's worth cultivating for everyday use! Gratitude is many things: a feeling, an attitude, a practice, a way of life.

A FEELING

Amazing things happen in the brain and body when we experience the feeling of gratitude. Gratitude opens our hearts. Research has shown that feeling grateful can literally shift our hearts into a healthy heart frequency.

When we feel grateful, our brains flood with chemicals—endorphins—that make us feel good. It's also true that we can't feel grateful and have a negative emotion such as anger or fear at the same time. That's worth remembering!

An Attitude

When we cultivate an attitude of gratitude, it expands our world and attracts people to us. Blaming, complaining, and judging contract our world, making us less attractive and more isolated. We can "act as if" in developing an attitude of gratitude. We can love even when we don't feel loving and be kind even when we'd rather be surly. In a neat twist, an attitude of gratitude often shifts our feelings.

A Practice

Pessimists are people who have exercised their muscles of negativity and sense of lack until those muscles are very strong. Optimists are people who have developed their gratitude muscles. The real gift is when, through practice, gratitude becomes a way of life.

It strikes me that experiencing gratitude for small things may be the only way to thrive and remain cheerful in the long haul, through the big difficulties of our individual and collective lives. Often gratitude for small things brings us right to the present moment. The past may be painful, the future murky, but here, now, right at this minute, I might be having an absolutely delicious cup of coffee. Or a neighbor brings me a cartoon, and I'm tickled and laugh, grateful for the small and precious moment of sharing.

A WAY OF LIFE

As mentioned above, gratitude actually releases chemicals in the brain that help us stay well and upbeat. Getting into the habit of being grateful can actually change your life. Try it.

Coaching Tips and Questions

I encourage you to develop your gratitude muscles until they are strong and automatic. Here are some things that will help:

- Count your blessings! Stop right now and write down at least 10 things you're genuinely grateful for. Include small things and large, such as the fact that you woke up this morning, that you are loved, that the sun is shining, that you love many people, that strawberries are in season, the support you get from others, your devoted dog, etc.
- Consider keeping a gratitude journal. Use any spiral notebook, or check online for a journal especially for keeping track of what you're grateful for.
- Think of someone in your life who annoys you. Now think of two things about that person for which you are grateful. Notice how quickly a feeling can change depending on what you focus on.
- If you have trouble thinking of things you're grateful for, be ridiculous. Be grateful for bad things that haven't happened—you don't have Alzheimer's, for example.

- Start a meeting by sharing points of gratitude. Include progress on projects, and help received from various people both in and out of the room. You'll be amazed at the positive energy this generates.

- Read *Attitudes of Gratitude, How to Give and Receive Joy Every Day of Your Life,* by M.J. Ryan.

3-16

COMFORT ZONES

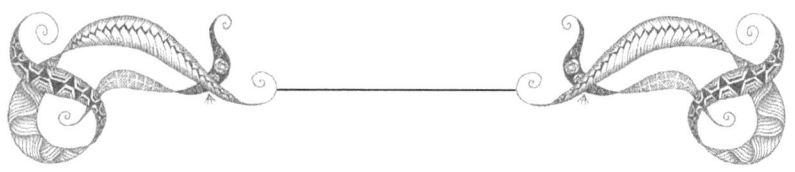

In the long-term we would be more happy with lives just outside of our comfort zone.
— Brandon A. Trean

IT'S A GOOD THING WE HAVE COMFORT ZONES, those ways of acting and thinking that do not cause us stress or require much thought. Comfort zones include those things we've learned to do that allow us to move through our days without constantly asking, "What next?" We gravitate toward what has become comfortable or familiar.

When I worked in drug and alcohol treatment, one of the things patients often said was that as lousy as their lives had become, they were familiar. Getting sober and living in greater light sounded good, but it was so unfamiliar it was scary. It was out of their comfort zones.

In *The Bigger Game*, Laura Whitworth and Rick Tamblyn say, "All comfort zones have some kind of benefit and some kind of cost attached to them." The essential point is that if we want to play a bigger game in life, if we want to grow, we're going to have to identify our comfort zones and leave behind those that don't serve us.

Whitworth and Tamblyn identify two types of comfort zones: habits of action and habits of thinking. Habits of action include never missing a particular TV show, eating certain foods, always brushing your teeth, and reacting by yelling when something doesn't go your way. Habits of thinking might include noticing what's going well, feeling grateful for small things, focusing on what's going wrong, finding fault with others, and feeling inadequate to many tasks. Habits that include both action and thinking include the roles we gravitate toward in our lives. We may find ourselves repeatedly playing the caretaker, the expert, the general, the free spirit, the martyr, or some other role.

The irony is that we develop comfort zones to keep ourselves safe and happy, yet over time, these habits actually devolve us to a state of boredom and complacency. So if we're interested in growing, having more meaning in our lives, or succeeding at a new level, we need to

- Identify our comfort zones
- Ask whether or not our comfort zone is serving us

The trouble is that we are usually blind to our comfort zones. They're so familiar to us we think they ARE us. Whitworth and Tamblyn say, "The fact is that unexamined comfort zones run our lives."

The good news is that when we actually do identify and step outside a comfort zone, we build a new comfort zone with greater capacity. The more we do this, the more we grow, the more we're able to accomplish, and the better we feel about ourselves.

This whole idea of looking at your comfort zones may be interesting but not make any difference in your life, unless there is a vision or a dream big enough to pull you out of that comfort zone. For me, the goal of staying healthy to enjoy my children and grandchildren keeps me walking outside even when the weather is cold. My friend Krishna is leaving a good job he's had for years because he's written a book that is changing people's lives. He wants to share that message broadly through workshops and webinars. (See *Beyond The Pig and the Ape* by Krishna Pendyala.)

What is your reason to move out of a comfort zone? Where might the benefit be greater than the cost?

Here are some final words of encouragement from Whitworth and Tamblyn:

> *If this chapter makes it seem that leaving comfort zones in the service of your Bigger Game is a grim slog, let us correct that impression here and now. Leaving comfort zones—and learning all the new ways you can step up to what matters most—is seriously delightful. The pleasure of channel surfing doesn't come remotely close to the fulfillment of discovering what you're made of and seeing what you're capable of doing.*

Coaching Tips and Questions

- Begin to notice your comfort zones. Ask yourself in each case, "What is the benefit? What is the cost?"
- Get conscious about when you're in a comfort zone and ask yourself, "Do I want to stay here?"
- Identify someone you can engage as an ally to help you identify the comfort zones you can't see.
- Develop strategies for moving beyond particularly damaging or high-cost comfort zones.
- List three bold actions can you take to examine and leave your comfort zones.

- For fun, check out your zones at www.WhatIsMyComfortZone.com?

3-17

AGING WELL

So far—this is the oldest I've been.
— George Carlin

WHEN MY DAD TURNED 90, we had a splendiferous celebration of his life. People came from far and wide, paying tribute to a life well lived. There was a band and a slide show. For many people, my dad serves as a model of positive thinking, integrity, generosity, and the value of persistent work. I got my basic ideas about management and running a business from watching Dad manage a robust insurance agency from an office in the back of our home.

After the celebration was over, it occurred to me that we missed a big piece: current reality. How do you live well at age 90, when it is hard to walk because of a stroke 12 years ago and you are legally blind? Well, here's how my dad does it.

- He's interested in others
- He appreciates every little kindness
- He loves to learn, watches documentaries and Dr. Phil
- He loves a good joke—and laughs heartily
- He's touched by a good story, and lets a tear fall

- He loves and appreciates my mom and says so
- He remembers the good times and shares them when asked
- He enjoys good food
- He doesn't whine or complain

Notice that the words "love" and "appreciation" come up repeatedly in this short list. Maybe the clue to aging well is to continue to love and appreciate.

Coaching Tips and Questions

- What is your definition of aging well?
- Describe someone you know who is aging well.
- What shifts in your life will help ensure you will age well?
- In what ways can you demonstrate love and appreciation in the upcoming week?
- Remember the old saying: It's never too late to have a great rest of your life.

Chapter 4

Stay Energized

STAY ENERGIZED

Seek above all for a game worth playing. Play as if your life and sanity depend on it, because they do!
– Robert de Ropp

CARS NEED GAS AND OIL TO RUN. That's their energy. If they run out of gas or oil, they stop. They can't go anywhere.

We need energy to keep going too. When we run out of energy, we don't stop like a car, but both our functioning and our enjoyment are compromised. When my energy is low, it is hard to get going, do the things I love, and be the person I want to be. When I run out of energy, I get crabby, think poorly, and sometimes take it out on people around me.

Many people have energy sometimes. But wouldn't it be nice to have energy you could count on? Energy helps us think well. Energy helps us be engaged in relationships. Since life is better when we feel energized, it makes sense to pay attention to how our energy flows. Many things can make a difference. For instance, it's worth paying attention to what saps your energy. Certain feelings? People? Food? Habits? And what increases your energy? Certain feelings? People? Food? Habits?

The essays in this section explore many things that help grow and sustain energy. Some of them may surprise you, such as the connection between how you breathe and the energy you feel. Maybe you never thought your breathing was something that you could improve to increase energy. But you can! How about your thoughts? Or how you manage emotions? Guess what? Thoughts and emotions make a huge difference in the energy department as well.

The essays in this section look at energy in many different ways, examining how setting goals and feeling passionate about them can increase energy. We'll look at the impact of humor on energy, and how the care and feeding of too much STUFF can drain our energy. We'll talk about building habits that cultivate energy, as well as ways of planning and thinking that can keep our energy steady through tough situations. We'll visit the connections between exercise and energy and sleep and energy.

I invite you to give careful answers to the coaching questions and try some of the tips you'll find in these essays. Since energy builds on itself, you can start anywhere; you will gain momentum from there. Nurturing sustained energy is one of the best gifts you can give yourself and the people in your life.

4-1
GOALS THAT INSPIRE

Motivation is an external, temporary high that pushes you forward. Inspiration is a sustainable internal glow which pulls you forward.
— Thomas Leonard

IN THE EARLY 1990'S BARBARA WAUGH, Human Resources Director, was asked by Joel Birnbaum, Director of Hewlett-Packard Laboratories, to work full-time on making HP Labs the "World's Best Industrial Research Labs" (WBIRL project). She asked employees from all over the world, "So what should be our vision?"

After a year of getting input, one engineer finally answered, "Best industrial research lab IN the world doesn't do it for me. I'd get up in the morning to be best FOR the world." With a change of one little word, the excitement became electric.

A senior engineer created a picture of what "FOR THE WORLD" meant to him: a famous picture of Bill Hewlett and Dave Packard gazing into the garage where it all started, now suddenly with the beautiful blue earth, taken from the Apollo spacecraft, inside the garage. This became their iconic poster. Eventually 50,000 employees purchased this poster on T-shirts, mugs, and mouse pads. "HP for the

World" became the banner uniting all the HP businesses and uniting the legacy of Bill and Dave to the present efforts. This tipped off a large-scale transformation of the company. People were inspired to perform. (Read the whole story in *The Soul in the Computer: The Story of a Corporate Revolutionary* by Barbara Waugh.)

I want to share a kind of goal that has made a huge difference to me. In the Arbinger Choice in Coaching course we call it an Out-of-the-Box goal. It is not just about me improving in some way—it is about me improving in relationship with others. It inspires because it pulls me to be bigger, to honor others, to be a better person FOR others. The HP shift from IN THE WORLD to FOR THE WORLD is a perfect example. Here are a couple of my own:

Examples

- For years, I wanted to become a great soup cook. I bought soup books but didn't start making soup. I got a soup pot but it didn't help. Finally, I changed the goal: "Share soup and stories with others." That one got me moving. I made soup and invited myself to lunch with a neighbor who was a new, snowed-in mother. I began inviting people over for soup and stories. Now I can't stop making soup and sharing it!

- I have had trouble sustaining an exercise program. It has always felt like a "should," even though when I do exercise, I have more energy. Finally, I changed the goal to: "Exercise to have more energy for family and friends." That totally shifted exercise for me. Now I prioritize exercise. I don't make excuses. I exercise because I want to.

And I DO have more energy for family and friends.

I love the distinction in the opening quote that Leonard makes between motivation and inspiration. Shifting a goal from a push, "have to" structure, to a pull, "want to" structure is magical! When it's only about me, excuses are easy. When others are affected, I am inspired to action.

Coaching Tips and Questions

- How can you create a goal that is big enough to inspire you, to get you out of bed in the morning?
- How can you change a goal or a New Year's Resolution so it includes and honors other people?
- How can you revise a goal so that it makes you a more responsive person, rather than just a more successful one?
- Who might help you move toward this new goal? It could be a friend, family member, or someone who does what you want to. (A regular jogger by my house, rain or shine, showed me weather doesn't have to be an excuse not to exercise.)

4-2
NOTICING

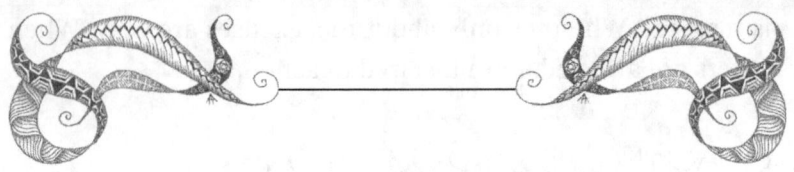

All there is to thinking is seeing something noticeable, which makes you see something you weren't noticing, which makes you see something that isn't even visible.

– Leo Strauss

It amazes me how blind I am—I stop seeing things: clutter; my cat Bonkers' messy toy basket; pictures on the wall. I'm startled when something wakes me up and I suddenly notice. Perhaps this blindness is the brain's gift so we can get on with life and not stay concerned about things that don't matter much.

Every year I complete a 19-day Bahá'í Fast. Every March for 19 days, we don't eat or drink anything between sunrise and sunset. I used to think the Fast was a dreadful inconvenience, at the least. Other times I thought it was torture. Somehow, over the years, its meaning has changed and, although it takes some mental and spiritual preparation, now the Fast is not hard, and I actually like it. The Fast jolts my routines, and I see many things I've been blind to. I watch the sunrise, and enjoy noting that the time of sunrise doesn't change evenly. Some days it's one minute earlier, some days two. The morning bird symphony is loud! On my walk one day a whole street of trees were in full bloom. The day before the branches had been just sticks.

When I take the first sip of water at sunset, it is glorious and I think it is the first time I've ever really tasted water. I nearly swooned over a nut yesterday.

This heightened awareness, this keen noticing that seems to come with fasting, makes me wonder how many other things in my life I'm blind to. Once, I wrote an e-mail to a client. His response showed confusion. As I was patiently responding, it occurred to me to reread my initial e-mail. I was shocked. My e-mail made no sense at all. How often am I blind to myself? Blaming the other person for what may well be my flaws?

I like the quote from Leo Strauss, above, because it follows the whole path from being blind and not knowing it, to seeing, and then beyond, to seeing what can't be seen. Maybe the biggest invisible thing that people can "see" is the condition of each other's heart. If someone is acting sweetly, but underneath they're angry, I know. What I want to notice, though, is when I'm the one who's offering a mixed message. I want to notice myself and the condition of my heart, and keep it peaceful—even when I'm not fasting.

It amazes me, but noticing more increases my energy. What a simple way to get more energy! One reason for this may be that this simple act of being a noticer helps me be the person I want to be.

Coaching Tips and Questions

- In your life, where might you be blind?
- How might you jumpstart your noticing by changing some routine?

- Think of a relationship or situation about which you're unhappy. Get curious about yourself in that relationship or situation. Really explore who you bring to it. What do you notice?

4-3

ENOUGH

There comes a point where having more than we need becomes a burden.
— Lynne Twist

IN DECLUTTERING MY OFFICE RECENTLY, I realized that all the stuff I have saved—because I might need it one day—crowds both my office and my head.

Many of us are living a paradox. We feel as if we have too little time; too little energy; too little money; not enough love, sex, beauty, or creativity. And we are aware of diminishing amounts of clean air and water in our lives. Yet we have too many clothes; too many toys, gadgets, and knickknacks; too much food; too much stuff. Is there a connection between these scarcities on the one hand and excess on the other?

I was deeply touched when I heard Lynne Twist (*The Soul of Money*) speak. She thinks that a primary driver today is a prevailing belief in scarcity. Twist was mentored by the great futurist and humanist, R. Buckminster Fuller, who taught an amazing and not-yet-believed truth.

In 1976, Fuller said that at this point in human evolution, we can choose to move from a you-or-me world—a world where either you win or I win—to a you-and-me world, where all of us have enough food, enough water, enough land, enough housing, and enough of the fundamental things for each one of us to live a fulfilling and productive life. Bucky, as he was called, also predicted that it would take us 50 to 100 years to make the required shift in the way we think and relate to ourselves and the world to grasp this truth.

Lynne Twist calls the idea of enough "exquisite," because our needs are met precisely:

> *When you let go of trying to get more of what you don't really need, it frees up oceans of energy to make a difference with what you have. And when you make a difference with what you have, it expands.*

The truth is that most of us don't know much about "enough." We don't know when we've had enough to eat or drink, when we've worked enough, bought enough clothes or toys. We always seem to want more. And wanting more keeps us from enjoying what we have. Mary Poppins said, "Enough is as good as a feast!"

According to Twist, when we let go of trying to get more, we recognize that our needs are always met in miraculous ways. Her words make me remember all the times as a young mother when I lost sleep because I didn't know how we'd pay the bills or buy food. Yet—it IS a miracle—somehow the bills got paid and we didn't starve! I'm thinking this idea of "enough" is the doorway to a much greater peace of mind. Twist offered several ways to practice sufficiency. I pass them on with a few of my own.

Coaching Tips and Questions

- De-clutter your life—at least once a week for one hour.

- Realize that everything you bring into your life requires care and feeding. Think of this when you contemplate buying something new.

- Practice appreciation. For example, tell someone three things you appreciate about him/her. Tell the clerk at the post office and the grocery store that you appreciate the service.

- When you give gifts, give intangibles. For example, give quality time. Give a gift certificate for an overnight trip, three hours of gardening, or time spent doing something the recipient needs or loves.

- Begin every meal with appreciation of where the food came from, and pay attention to that moment when your body has had exactly enough.

- Go through your checkbook and your credit card bills. Be more conscious of what you use, consume, and spend.

- Contribute money to things you believe in and truly care about.

4-4

Ten Delicious Daily Habits

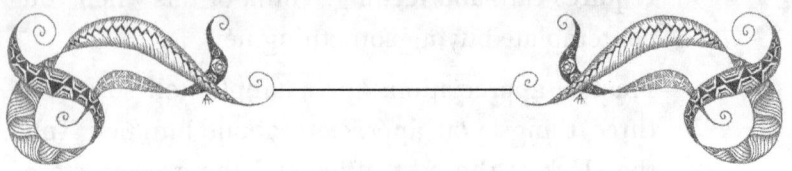

Good habits, once established, are just as hard to break as bad habits.

— Robert Puller

MANY YEARS AGO WHEN I WAS IN TRAINING to be a coach through Coach U, we were taught the value of creating and using 10 daily habits. The promise was that if we actually named 10 things we loved to do, and then figured out a way to build them into our day, we'd be healthy, focused, energetic, balanced, and feel good! An attractive promise.

I took the challenge and it worked. Then over the years, I sort of forgot. But I'm back to it now and finding it so delicious! Each day is improved when it is bookended by happy rituals, and there is a treat in the middle.

Here's my Current List of 10 Delicious Daily Habits

1. Begin and end the day reading from the Bahá'í Writings or other holy scriptures.
2. Practice 30 minutes of Yoga/Chi Kung.

3. Have a relaxed cup of coffee and read something inspirational.
4. Have meaningful connections with at least two people.
5. Enjoy a mid-afternoon cup of tea.
6. Limit news to 20 minutes.
7. Nap.
8. Perform one act of kindness.
9. Exercise aerobically for 30 minutes (walk/bike).
10. Write daily in a gratitude journal.

I've been doing these for a couple of months, so they're coming easily. And I DO feel good: focused, energized, and balanced!

Coaching Tips and Questions

- What would you include in a list of 10 delicious daily habits, even if some of them seem difficult to build into your day?
- Choose habits you WANT to do. No "shoulds" or "coulds". Choose things you love to do but often forget or don't find time for.
- Choose habits that GIVE you energy. This might mean doing something—like eating 6 fruits and veggies a day—or stopping something—like watching television or eating after 7 p.m.
- What habits are easy to include because you already do them?

- Modify your 10 daily habits as needed. Don't be a slave to them. Some may not work, so find others. If you get tired of one habit, replace it with another.
- When will you start living the new habits on the list? How will you remind yourself while they're becoming habitual?

4-5

Hurrying

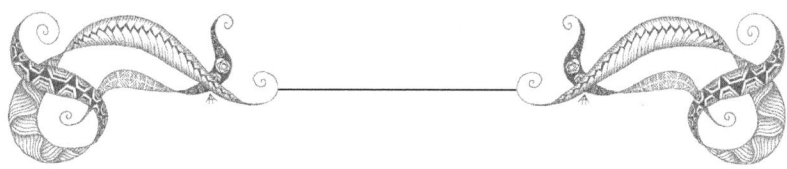

I regret less the road not taken than my all-fired hurry along the road I took.
— Robert Brault

HURRYING IS A HABIT, one I seem to have cultivated to a fine art. I'm always hurrying to get a lot of things done before I hurry somewhere to do a lot of other things. When I'm hurrying, I often miss things. I know this because every now and then I slow down. One day my friend Sallie invited me to take an early morning stroll through the Village of Sewickley, where I live. There were so many new shops and beautiful flowers I hadn't noticed on my nearly daily drives through this village I was amazed! I had to ask myself, "What else am I missing?"

The answer came when I was taking care of my 16-month-old granddaughter, Fianna. After we'd eaten and played awhile and had some milk, it was time to go to bed. I rocked her and put her in the crib, and Fianna screamed. I picked her up and rocked her a bit more, then put her back and she cried again. I suddenly realized that while I wasn't done with caring for Fianna, I had moved on in my head, hurrying to some quite unimportant task that called me. I picked her up and smiled, and said to her aloud, "There's nowhere I'd rather be than with you." And I sat in the rocker and loved her with all my heart. I was just right there with Fianna, not somewhere else. She fell asleep in a nanosecond, and I was energized by having slowed down.

Sometimes the hurrying habit is so strong that I forget what's really important to me. Annie Lamott says, "Be where your feet are." When I'm hurrying, I am always on my way to somewhere else. Not right where my feet are.

Have you ever tried to hurry others? I have. The recipients of my hurrying strategies have mostly been husbands and children. The results are almost always the same—they slow way down! One time when my son Gordon was in the 2nd grade and not wanting to get up for school, I physically got him up and dressed him, chiding all the while about how we needed to hurry. By the time I had gone into the other room for something, he put his PJs back on and was snuggled in bed with the blankets pulled up. When I think about how it must be to live with me—someone who hurries so much—it makes me tired.

All the hurrying we do fails to get us ahead anyway. Recently, I was driving into Pittsburgh when a car whizzed past me. He darted in behind one car after another, weaving to get wherever he was going faster. I was amused to notice when we got to a stop light several miles down the road, he was right in front of me. The hurrying had not given him an edge. Maybe he enjoyed it, maybe the hurrying made this man feel important, or maybe it made him anxious. I don't know.

Lao Tzu said something worth pondering: "Nature does not hurry, yet everything is accomplished."

Coaching Tips and Questions

- If you have the hurrying habit, think of three things you can do to slow it down just enough to notice more.

- How could you "be where your feet are" more often?

- Consider this quote from Cheryl Richardson: "To do what you really, really want, you may have to say "no" to what you really want."

- What might you say "no" to?

- Swear off hurrying for one day. Do everything slightly slower. See if, like in nature, everything is still accomplished.

4-6

NAVIGATING YOUR EXPERIENCE

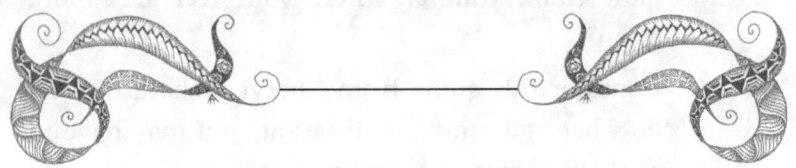

> *All we require to successfully navigate the quality of an experience is to predetermine how we are going to feel about it once we have passed through it.*
>
> – Michael Brown

MY UNCLE BUDDY IS AN 85-YEAR-OLD, ECCENTRIC HERMIT. He prefers no visitors, but when I couldn't reach him on the phone, I decided a visit was in order. Since he lives in California only a couple hundred miles from where I would be spending Christmas, I planned a three-day visit.

I knew the experience would be challenging, so I used the Navigating Your Experience model described by Michael Brown. I have found it to be a simple, profound method for moving successfully through all kinds of situations, from challenging phone calls to major presentations. Brown, an unknown Australian, used this method to get his book, *The Presence Process*, published by a major publisher.

Here's how it goes: You decide how you want to feel when you've successfully completed whatever it is you're working on. The feeling is important, because you come back to it anytime during the process when things get difficult. Then you plan the details of what you're going to do. Then you do it.

Brown ties his model to developmental stages:
1. *Emotional*—The feeling you want to have when the experience is over
2. *Mental*—The steps you'll take, or the plan
3. *Physical*—Doing it

Brown says we never would have grown up if we'd skipped #1 and moved straight into #2 as babies!

So here's how the process worked in my visit with Uncle Buddy. Before we went (husband Hal went with me for moral support), I got very clear about how I wanted to feel at the end of the three days. I'll use words here, but what I wanted was the FEELING of reconnection with Uncle Buddy, the feeling that I had been helpful, and the assurance he was safe and cared for, at least for now.

Hal and I had to bang on Uncle Buddy's window to wake him. Since he lives mostly on Rice Krispy Treats and milk, with occasional visits to Burger King, Buddy is gaunt, to say the least. He's stopped shaving and cutting his hair, so he looks like a wild man, but he greeted us warmly. He had trouble understanding why his apartment needed to be cleaned. His lamps were all broken, so he had only one functioning light bulb. His refrigerator had died. Rather than allow myself to become overwhelmed, I went back to the way I wanted to feel when the visit was over. I kept enjoying the small moments of reconnection we experienced over and over. We were able to get the apartment cleaned, buy new lamps and a new refrigerator.

When, 15 minutes before we planned to leave, Uncle Buddy's hot water heater began spewing steam and hot water, I was glad I had that feeling to hold onto. When two big fire trucks arrived, and all the neighbors came around to offer help and see what was going on, Uncle Buddy sat in his rocker smiling. I had navigated the experience successfully. The fire trucks were just a bonus!

The Process in a Nutshell

1. Imagine the way you want to FEEL when you've successfully navigated the experience.
2. Make a plan
3. Do it
4. When difficulties arise, as they will, go back in your mind to #1

Coaching Tips and Questions

- Where might you try navigating your experience?
    - In response to a challenging situation?
    - To meet a goal?
    - To run a great meeting?
    - To complete a difficult conversation or phone call?
    - To have a wonderful day?
- Once you've chosen where and when to try Brown's process, carefully walk through the steps. You won't know how well this process works until you try it!

4-7
Choices

The way you spend your time is the way you spend your life.
– Charles Hobbs

WHEN I FIRST HEARD THIS QUOTE, I was stopped short. The point is obvious. But some uncomfortable truth lurks just under the surface. I think it is this: Every minute of every day we make choices about what to do and how to do it, what to think and how to think. The implications are big! We usually do not recognize or experience all these choice points. When we do, it is freeing (and sometimes terrifying).

Examples
- Choose not to do a task at all.
- Choose to change the way you think about someone or something.
- Choose to sit quietly for 10 minutes before choosing.
- Choose to worry about something.
- Choose not to worry.
- Choose to advocate for something you believe in.

- Choose to eat healthy food.
- Choose to be kind.
- Choose to leave a safe career to follow a dream.
- Realize you have a choice even when you feel you don't.

Mark, a successful and driven entrepreneur, recently ruptured a disk in his neck. Forced to slow down, he made a choice to stop working at night. Suddenly there was delicious balance in his life—time to play with his son, enjoy leisure with his wife, visit with his neighbors. As is often true, the injury served as a wake-up call. Mark continued to choose this delicious balance when he fully recovered. It was a life-altering choice he wasn't even aware he had.

Coaching Tips and Questions

- Go through your day noticing the choices you are making.
- Ask yourself, "Are these the choices I really want?"
- Ask yourself, "Is this the way I want to spend my life?"
    - If not, choose again.
    - Don't wait for the pain of a wake-up call.
    - Be bold.

4-8
HUMOR

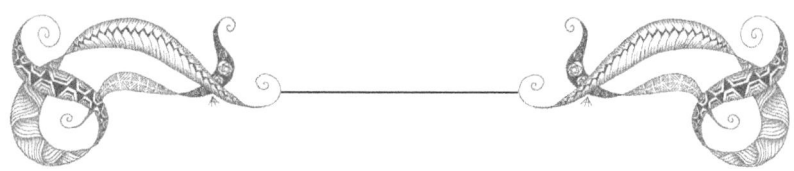

Humor is mankind's greatest blessing.
— Mark Twain

DRIVING ON A LONG ROAD TRIP, I grew sleepy. An interesting CD I was listening to blurred into the background. When chewing gum and drinking coffee didn't help, I stopped and found a book on tape by David Sedaris called *Holiday on Ice*. The very first essay described his stint as a department store Christmas elf. I laughed so heartily that I was suddenly wide awake!

Laughing at David Sedaris as an elf reminded me of the time my daughter Lisa got a job at Wendy's. The first day she blew up balloons for hours. Then they gave her the Wendy costume and sent her into the bathroom to change. She went into the bathroom and climbed out the window. That was her first and last day of work at Wendy's. Picturing that teenager climbing out the window instead of wearing a Wendy's costume had me laughing again. Humor can be so therapeutic!

When my parents were in their 90s, I talked with them on the phone every night. Sometimes there wasn't much to talk about, so I shared jokes with them. Even when their memories were failing, they responded immediately to many jokes, and the laughter had a calming, healing effect. Usually what tickled was a slight twist, something they didn't see coming. Here's one they liked:

> What do you get when you cross an abalone with a crocodile?
>
> When you do it right, you get an abadile. When you do it wrong, you get a crocobalone.

Mahatma Gandhi said, "If I had no sense of humor, I would long ago have committed suicide." Humor is really a way of seeing, of putting things into perspective. It makes us more resilient. Henry Ward Beecher got it right when he said, "A person without a sense of humor is like a wagon without springs. It's jolted by every pebble on the road."

People who are easy with humor see comedy even in seemingly impossible situations. And the great news is that when we laugh, it registers in our body's chemistry, reversing unhealthy stress reactions. The bad news is that many of us forget to use humor, to laugh often.

The average child laughs 400 times per day, the average adult 15 times. How did we lose those 385 laughs? How can we cultivate humor? Laugh more?

Coaching Tips and Questions

- Several times a day, look for what might be humorous. See the ironic in the difficult.
- Imagine you're looking down on a situation from 10,000 feet. Given a little distance, what can you see to laugh at?
- Read some jokes. Garrison Keillor's many joke books are just silly enough. You might also subscribe to some daily joke online. (There are lots of

them, some cleaner than others, so I leave you to your own devices.)

- Find or start a local laughter club. Check out www.LaughterYoga.org for ideas.

4-9
ATTENTION NOT ENERGY

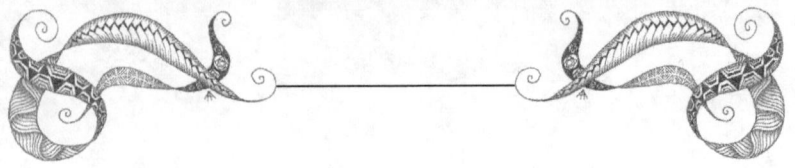

When you face something unpleasant, give it your attention but not your energy.

– Charles Hobbs

THIS QUOTE DELIVERS SOME OF THE BEST ADVICE I've ever received. I understand it to mean, "Don't waste emotional energy." How often do we get all upset, costing ourselves lots of energy, only to discover we've made things worse instead of better?

Here's how you can put this advice to work. When you face an unpleasant situation, such as

- Your computer crashes;
- You have to work with someone you don't like;
- You can't find something;
- You have so much to do you feel totally overwhelmed; or
- You make a big mistake,

say to yourself, "Here's a situation that deserves my attention but not my energy. I am just not going to get all worked up about it, because it won't help. Instead I'll give the situation my attention and respond one step at a time."

There are two parts to this strategy:
1. *Notice that you are in an unpleasant situation.* Many of us move through the world without noticing. Clues might be the tightening of your neck, jaw, or belly—a feeling of rising upset, even panic—or becoming reactive to everyone and everything around you.

2. *Give the situation attention without emotional energy.* This gets easier with practice. Some practice ideas that can help you focus your attention without energy include paying conscious attention to each step as you walk; concentrating on each movement as you mow the lawn or cook, and noticing exactly where you are minute-to-minute as you drive.

Coaching Tips and Questions

- Practice noticing when you are anxious or beginning to get anxious. Pay attention to the physical tightening clues.

- When you notice that you are in one of those situations where you know you could get all upset, wasting emotional energy, talk to yourself, saying, "This is one of those times that calls for attention, not energy."

- Give the situation your full attention, but keep the downward slide at bay by refusing to give it your emotional energy.

- Respond one step at a time, noticing that you are getting through it without all the usual upset!

4-10

PLAY

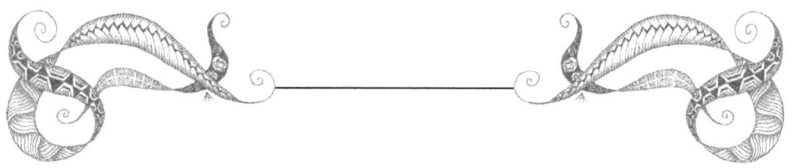

> *The truly great advances of this generation will be made by those who can make outrageous connections, and only a mind which knows how to play can do that.*
>
> — Nagle Jackson

PLAY IS REALLY IMPORTANT. Many of us who are silly at heart have known this all along, but it's satisfying to have it verified by people who study things like survival and the advancement of civilizations.

Stuart Brown, M.D., founder of The National Institute for Play (www.nifplay.org) tells a story in his 2009 book, *Play, How It Shapes the Brain, Opens the Imagination, and Invigorates the Soul*. The story is about a hungry young polar bear who approached Hudson, a sled dog. Warm weather had prevented ice from forming, so the polar bears had been unable to hunt and eat seals. Musher Brian La Doone and his party watched the approach with dread, knowing the rambunctious Hudson was no match for the polar bear. However, the unexpected happened.

As the polar bear closed in, Hudson did not bark or flee. Instead, he wagged his tail and bowed, a classic play signal. The polar bear responded, and together dog and bear wrestled and played rough and tumble in the snow for 15 minutes. They played so energetically that at one point the bear had to lie down, belly up, a universal sign in the animal kingdom for a time-out. More astonishing still, the polar bear reappeared around the same time on each of 5 days to engage in a romp with the dog. By that time the ice had frozen and the polar bear could eat. Brown concluded that sometimes play is more important than food.

Brown defines play as a state of mind rather than an activity. Play, he says, is "an absorbing, apparently purposeless activity that provides enjoyment and a suspension of self-consciousness and sense of time. It is self-motivating and makes you want to do it again."

Writing is play to me but some people experience writing as work. We must each identify for ourselves what is "play" for us. And it is important that we do. When we have played, our brains work better and we are more energized, optimistic, and creative.

In the development of young children and animals, play is essential for learning who to befriend or avoid, and how to recognize social cues. When we observe young children playing or watching an *Animal Planet* video, we often smile and re-experience the delicious feeling of play.

Interestingly Dr. Brown, a retired psychiatrist, first focused on play in 1966, after noting the absence of play in a mass murderer, Charles Whitman, whom he'd been asked by the governor of Texas to study. Whitman had continually had his natural tendency to play suppressed by an oppressive and abusive father. This alerted Brown to the possibility that play might be very important to health. He went on to study many mass murderers, and repeatedly found abnormal or absent play histories in this group. This led eventually to his founding of the National Institute for Play, which takes very seriously the goal of understanding the role of play in our individual and collective lives.

I am lucky to have a family that really knows how to play. I remember a week we spent together, where we played trampoline dodgeball, ultimate Frisbee, bocce ball, homemade Pictionary (Eakes-sionary), and self-organizing jam sessions with singing and many instruments.

In addition to piano, guitar, and drum, we had triangle, sheep's toenail shaker, thumb cymbals, and others. My 10-year-old granddaughter, Ruthie, shared her silver glitter fingernail polish with everyone, including the boys and men. We sat around talking, reading, napping, telling stories, and laughing in naturally forming groups. It was a time of great renewal and refreshment for me.

Dr. Brown says:
> *I don't think it is too much to say that play can save your life. Life without play is a grinding, mechanical existence organized around doing the things necessary for survival. Play is the basis of all art, games, books, sports, movies, fashion, fun, and wonder—in short, the basis of what we think of as civilization. Play is the vital essence of life. It is what makes life lively.*

COACHING TIPS AND QUESTIONS

- What is fun for you? How can you plan to do more of that in the next month?
- How can you be more playful generally? What tickles your funny bone?
- Who in your life brings out the playful side of you? Call that person and plan a get together for a playful time together.

- In addition to you, who would be happy if you created more time for play in your life?
- What might a playful attitude liberate in you?

4-11

10-10-10 RULE

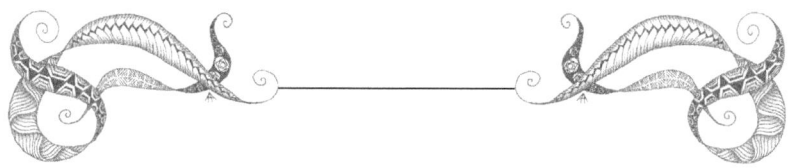

The real voyage of discovery consists not in seeking new landscapes but in having new eyes.
— Marcel Proust

NEW EYES? HOW DO WE GET NEW EYES? I often think of this wonderful quote from Proust when I see something from a new perspective or am thrilled, as if for the first time, by the sight of the blooming trees of spring. New eyes.

Yet now I want to be more literal. I have recently realized one cause of continual stress is tired, strained eyes.

Human eyes were not meant to focus on near-point activities like reading, working at a computer, or watching television for hours at a time. Our eyes stay healthiest and most elastic when they switch from flat, close work to distant, three-dimensional views frequently. That's where the 10-10-10 rule comes in. I know it sounds like lawn fertilizer, but in this case, it is eye fertilizer—a kind that we all need. Here's how it goes:

- While you are engaged in any near-point activity (anything requiring you to focus on an object within 7 feet), every 10 minutes focus on an object at least 10 feet away for 10 seconds.

- This may sound like a lot of work, but once you make it a habit, you will hardly notice you are doing it. And by doing it, you will relieve stress, allowing your ciliary muscle and lens to relax momentarily so that the eye does not adapt to the near-point condition, leading to a loss of distant vision. It also re-energizes you instead of draining you. Use the 10-10-10 Rule and teach it to your co-workers, children, friends, and family.

- If you work in a small room or cubicle, or it's dark outside, you can do the "Distant Night" exercise instead of the 10-10-10 Rule for 10 seconds. This also gives your eyes a break. Close your eyes while you imagine you're looking into the distant night. Your eyes relax as they imagine looking out at a distance. You'll find it even more relaxing if you warm your hands by rubbing them together and cupping them over your eyes while doing the Distant Night exercise, leaning your elbows on a table or your knees.

These exercises come from *Vision For Life* by Orlin G. Sorensen.

It's amazing how much relief you can get from doing these little exercises. Because all our body parts are connected, when our eyes are tired and strained, our whole body feels it. When our eyes stay fresh, so does the rest of us. Try it.

Coaching Tips and Questions

- Start practicing the 10-10-10 Rule or Distant Night regularly, NOW.

- Put a sticky note or a piece of masking tape on your computer monitor that says 10-10-10 Rule as a reminder.
- Make a bookmark with 10-10-10 Rule on it to remind yourself to use this rule when you're reading a book.

4-12

Sleep

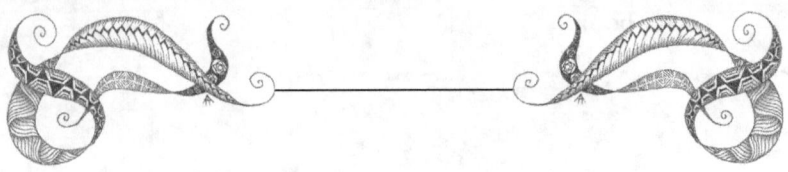

Without enough sleep, we all become tall two-year-olds.

– JoJo Jensen

Last week I observed a darling 3-year-old boy, Troy, having a meltdown in the check-out line at the supermarket. Troy kept loudly changing his mind about what he wanted. He was past comforting, thrashing in his mother's arms. The mother explained apologetically to the rest of us in the line, "Troy's overtired. He missed his nap."

As grown-ups, we've learned, for the most part, not to yell and thrash, but when we're overtired, we feel pretty much like Troy at the supermarket. I think of parents who work demanding, full-time jobs, and take kids to seemingly endless practices and games or meets. I think of busy executives, who never get enough sleep. I think of myself and many of my friends, who do so many good and interesting things with our lives that we are often frazzled.

Recent research shows that lack of sleep in adults:
- Impairs judgment
- Reduces "rapid cognition" or intuition

- Leaves us emotionally vulnerable, with less ability to contain our emotions

Thomas Dekker said, "Sleep is the golden chain that ties health and our bodies together."

Here are a couple of suggestions for getting more sleep:

Go to bed even though you haven't finished everything you need/want to do. Write yourself a clear note to remind yourself what you want to do. Set the alarm, and go to bed. When you wake up, you'll be able to accomplish the tasks much more easily than if you'd done them while tired.

Take a nap. Companies who have instituted short "Power Napping" policies claim greater productivity, fewer mistakes, and fewer accidents. James Mass, a Cornell University sleep researcher, says, "I've recommended napping to thousands of overtired executives."

I am a devoted napper. I find 15 minutes of sleep in the middle of the day refreshes me in an almost miraculous way! The list of famous nappers is long and includes Jim Lehrer, John F. Kennedy, Winston Churchill, Albert Einstein, Thomas Edison, Johannes Brahms, Napoleon Bonaparte, Leonardo da Vinci, and my grandpa Buckner.

It's never too late to start napping. Hal learned to nap after he was 60, and described naps as "deliciously restorative." If you haven't tried napping, I suggest you do, even if it's just shutting your eyes at your desk for 10 minutes during lunch.

Coaching Tips and Questions

- Do you get enough sleep to stay alert, productive, and in control of your emotions?
- If not, try one of these:
    - Go to bed at a set time each night, even if you haven't finished your work. Get up earlier instead of staying up later.
    - Get at least 30 minutes of good exercise during the day.
    - Don't watch TV just before falling asleep. Instead, try listening to soothing music and turning it off before you go to sleep.
    - Do not drink caffeine in the afternoon.
    - Limit your evening alcohol intake.
    - Sleep in a totally dark room.

4-13

DECAY IS OPTIONAL

You do have to age, but you don't have to rot.
— Chris Crowley and Henry Lodge

MY SISTER WENDY SENT ME A BOOK she said had changed her husband Gary's life. I was intrigued. I'd thought becoming a grandpa had done it. She said, "Yes and no." The book inspired Gary, generally conservative, to buy a sailboat to dock near the granddaughter, so they can see her often.

The book, titled *Younger Next Year*, is, indeed, a winner! My sister sent me the version for women. (The original is for men.) The full title is *Younger Next Year: Live Strong, Fit, and Sexy—Until You're 80 and Beyond*, by Chris Crowley and Henry Lodge, M.D. I've been so impacted by this book; I just have to recommend it to you. The quote above is the title of the first section of the book, "You Do Have to Age, but You Don't Have to Rot." That's great news for those of us who are getting up there in age! For a taste of the book, here are "Harry's Rules":

1. Exercise six days a week for the rest of your life.
2. Do serious aerobic exercise four days a week for the rest of your life.

3. Do serious strength training, with weights, two days a week for the rest of your life.
4. Spend less than you make.
5. Quit eating crap!
6. Care.
7. Connect and commit.

Okay, so what's new? What's new is that these guys are funny and full of scientific information. The writing is breezy and amazingly motivating. It's one thing to know we "should" do these things. It's another to feel that switch and WANT to. I'm actually getting up in the morning WANTING to do aerobic exercise. That's new. The miracle is how energetic I feel. How young!

Consider this gem on exercise, written by Crowley, who is over 70, and blunt:

> Nothing you are doing in the Next Third [season of life] is as important as daily exercise. It's deadly serious, because it will keep you from becoming a pathetic, dependent old fool.

He also tells us very directly that we're not tired at the end of our day because of too much exercise—but because of too little! He goes on to remind us that strength training has been shown to stop bone loss cold in multiple studies.

Crowley and Lodge recommend keeping a log. They suggest a simple journal in which you keep track of three things every day: What you eat; exactly what kind and how much exercise you got; and what you did with your day that you care about. Otherwise, they claim, you will lose command—of yourself.

I've often kept a journal, but never one like this. I discovered in just 10 days that I exercised less than I thought; ate more chocolate than I admitted; and spent more time than I thought doing things I don't care about. So, I've made some changes. Keeping this log is really helpful.

Check out the website www.YoungerNextYear.com. Or better yet, buy and read the book. I think you'll thank me.

Coaching Tips and Questions

- What kind and amount of exercise do you need to stay fit? And why?
- How can you eat well for continued health into old age?
- How much of your life centers on what you really care about?
- How many deep connections do you have with friends and family?

4-14

CELEBRATE!

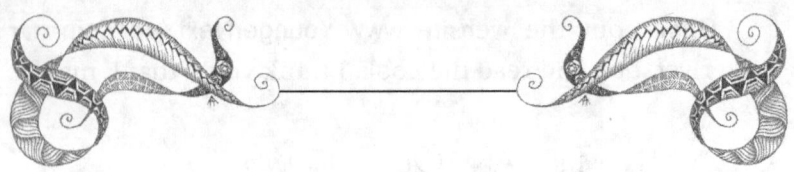

Celebrate what you want to see more of!
– Adage

In the work world, we are often so focused on problems that we don't stop to acknowledge, let alone celebrate, our many successes. When we take the small amount of time required to acknowledge and celebrate, it rewards, energizes, and motivates us to continue.

This works in personal life as well. Focusing on "small wins" for ourselves, in our families, and with friends leads to more wins and more energy.

Examples

- I remember when Jamie, my 1-year-old granddaughter, was just learning to walk down steps alone, holding onto the rail. One day she made her way down the steps, saying "big girl" aloud on each step. At the bottom, she looked up, smiled, and she and her whole family clapped and sang "Yeah!"
- A team in a high-tech manufacturing company was working on three projects. Two of the projects

had serious difficulties. One experienced a successful test run. The team took 10 minutes at the beginning of a team meeting to read comments from the pleased customer and celebrate what they had done well. Then they moved to the hard cases, feeling energized.

Coaching Tips and Questions

- Stop a moment each day to acknowledge and do a mini-celebration of your successes (smile at least.)
- Add "successes" or "small wins" as the first agenda item for team meetings. Acknowledge individuals and teams.
- Share with the other person any aspect of the relationship for which you're grateful. For example, "We have such fun bicycling together!"
- Periodically celebrate successes, in style.
- Make a big deal in your family about yours and others' successes. This is not only good for the family, but it is good modeling for children.
- Have a pizza party or take your team to lunch or a ballgame to celebrate a "win."

Chapter 5

See Connections Everywhere

SEE CONNECTIONS EVERYWHERE

At the heart of each of us, whatever our imperfections, there exists a silent pulse of perfect rhythm, a complex of wave forms and resonances, which is absolutely individual and unique, and yet which connects us to everything in the Universe.
– George Leonard

WE ARE AMAZINGLY INTERDEPENDENT, whether we realize it or not. When there is a drought in California, our food supply in the East is disrupted. When there is war in Iraq, the price of gas goes up in Pennsylvania. Having a splint on a broken finger on my right hand throws my whole system off. Volcanos that have spewed smoke thousands of miles away influence the weather in a faraway place.

A serious field of study, called Systems Thinking, studies this interdependence of things. In this context, a system is a set of at least two interacting elements that function as a complex whole. Examples of systems are bodies, families, computers, companies, politics, nations, and the solar system.

There are often systems within systems, as a classroom within a school is within a neighborhood within a city. Each is a system on its own, but also part of larger systems. And because these are all normal parts of our lives, the systems are often invisible to us. That can be a problem. We can't see what we can't see. So we may blame a person or a group when the problem is the system.

Systems Thinking is important as both a philosophy and a tool set, because it helps us see and understand our interdependence. When we understand some things about how systems work, we have a better idea of how to change them.

Knowing how to make changes in a system is important knowledge. Think of how often today's problems come from yesterday's "solutions." For example, a wonderful new medicine often solves one problem and causes another! If we got good at understanding this radical interdependence, we might predict the problems our "solutions" might cause, and make decisions with that broad picture in mind.

An amazing thing about this interconnected world is how a small change in one place can have a large effect somewhere else. You have probably heard of the butterfly effect. This is the theory that a single occurrence, no matter how small, can change the course of the universe forever. It got its name from the notion that the flap of a butterfly's wings changes the air around it so much that it could spawn a tornado two continents away. The science is more complicated than I can understand, but the message I take away is that we need to be more mindful of our thoughts and actions, because they have more influence than we realize!

Seeing all of these interconnections clearly is not popular, because such thinking is often complex and slows down decision-making. However, the payoff is huge. For example, at one point my husband, Hal, had 11 different doctors. The doctors did not talk to each other. We became concerned when some of the prescribed medicines seemed to fight each other.

A visit to the Mayo Clinic gave us a glimpse into what whole-person medicine might look like. One doctor coordinated Hal's care. Hal saw several doctors, and they talked to each other. They ended up taking him off several medications and prescribing something different so that the medicine worked best for Hal's whole body. It made a big difference!

It's important to look for connections on a small scale in our everyday lives and on a big, global scale as well. I was thrilled recently to read that the work of the Rocky Mountain Institute (RMI) has finally hit a tipping point. Since the 1970's, RMI has been working with a "whole-system approach" to develop efficient, sustainable, market-based energy solutions. More than twenty years ago RMI began promoting the compact fluorescent light bulb and hybrid cars. People laughed.

The essays in this section explore the interdependent nature of all people and all things. Reflecting on the essays may help you understand where you have power and where you don't. You may consider the ways in which you are always influencing and being influenced. I invite you to read with an eye to accept things as they are and also to intervene and change things in ways that have the best chance of success.

5-1
Maintaining Systems

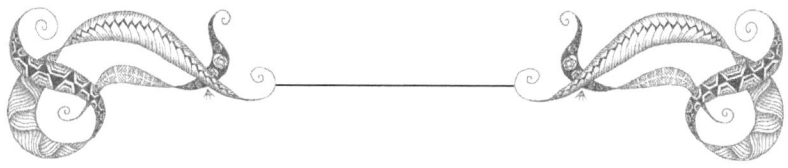

When we try to pick out anything by itself, we find it hitched to everything else in the universe.
– John Muir

I AM FASCINATED WITH SYSTEMS THAT WORK WELL. I like observing the systems around me—my car, my computer, my family, my body, my business, my grocery store. I notice that some systems work better than others.

As I observe systems, I see that it takes at least two steps to maintain them: Notice the system and maintain it. We have to begin by noticing the system. Barry Oshry says, "When we don't see systems we are at their mercy."

Then we need to maintain the system. Sometimes we need systems to maintain systems.

Some systems are easier to maintain than others. Cars, for instance, give us precise maintenance schedules. Then dealers remind us when it's time for a tune-up. Computers tell us when to update the virus definitions and defragment.

A system like a body, family, or company is a little harder. We tend to forget these are systems needing maintenance until we get sick or there is a blow up or a slowdown. Then we often respond with a quick fix that generates its own unintended consequences.

A system like a body, family, or company can best be maintained by paying attention to itself, noting changes, and purposefully adapting, and realigning the vision.

Example

My husband Hal experienced significant vision loss. This was a real change to his system. While we were actively looking for the cause, Hal kept up his voluminous reading by using a low vision machine and reading books on tape.

Our relationship also had to adapt. We kept the contents of the refrigerator in a certain order so he could find things easily. Hal had always been a fearless driver while I was not. Because I wanted to continue the adventuresome life we enjoyed together, I began boldly driving to unfamiliar places. Our system was under pressure and we were forced to pay more attention than ever to our own and each other's needs. The strain to the system was made easier because we'd practiced paying attention to our marriage, keeping it tuned.

Coaching Tips and Questions

- Identify 3 to 5 systems you're in.
- Ask, about each system, "How's it doing?"
- Maintain the systems in your life with loving care (your car, computer, body, and relationships). Adapt, realign, and evolve.

- If some system in your life is functioning poorly, ask, "How can I disrupt it?" Disruption is the only way to change a system.

5-2
MANAGING SYSTEM DELAYS

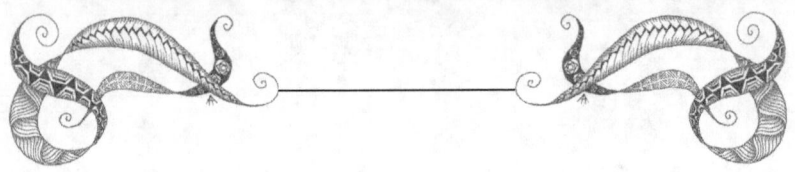

Argh! Help!

– Sharon Eakes

THOSE ARE THE SOUNDS I MADE ONE DAY, at the helm of our rented houseboat in the Everglades. A houseboat is slow to respond. It has a very different rhythm from power steering. Luckily, our houseboat had a GPS (Global Positioning System), which gave me a line to follow on a screen, and kept us from being hopelessly lost in the 10,000 Islands. I crossed the GPS line and headed into a mangrove swamp. Scared, I turned sharply in the other direction. I zigged and zagged, finding it impossible to wait long enough after each correction, needing to DO something: Fix it now!

Even when we understand systems—and know that delays are part of systems—it is hard to wait through a delay.

EXAMPLES

We live with frustrating system delays everywhere:
- Children moving through developmental stages
- Seasons of the year
- The creative process
- The stock market

- Software engineers writing workable programs
- Cycle time in manufacturing
- Response time in service industries

One of the known ways to optimize a system is to manage its delays. Here is a 3-part guide for managing system delays.

- Say the Serenity Prayer. This may seem corny, but it helps.
    > *God grant me the serenity*
    > *To accept the things I cannot change*
    > *The courage to change the things I can*
    > *And the wisdom to know the difference.*
- If a delay falls in the "cannot change" department, name it, respect it, and trust it. Then manage yourself. Sitting on my hands and breathing deeply eventually helped me stop overcorrecting the houseboat.
- If a delay CAN be shortened, AND it's important, then bring all available resources to bear on shortening it. The most significant reductions in cycle time and response time come from using the ideas and experience of all kinds of people involved in or affected by the delay, from both inside and outside an organization.

Coaching Tips and Questions

- Identify five system delays that are frustrating you right now.
- Categorize your five system delays identified above into either "cannot change" or "delay can be shortened."

- How will you manage yourself about the delays that cannot change? Remember the Serenity Prayer.
- For the delays that can be shortened, write a bulleted list of your plan to bring all resources to bear.

5-3
Living with Terrorism

The object of terrorism is terrorism.
— George Orwell

In response to my question, "How do you live with terrorism?" my friend Marilyn, who lives in Israel answered, "I build many, deep conversations into my life, and I don't spend much time thinking about the future."

I keep coming back to Marilyn's two responses. They are elegant in their simplicity.

Take the idea of many, deep conversations. What if we regularly talked deeply with our family members? What if we shared our thoughts and feelings and listened well to what is important to them? How different would our families be? What if we risked real conversations with our friends, neighbors, and co-workers? What would be different if we approached people who have perspectives different from ours with curiosity, openness? (If this idea intrigues you, you would like *Difficult Conversations, How to Discuss What Matters Most*, by Stone, Patton, and Heen.)

Consider the second suggestion. What if we gave up worrying about the future? What if we dropped the fear and the anxiety and asked instead, "If these were the last few minutes of my life, would I be pleased with them?"

Many slogans remind us to live in the moment. A couple of my favorites are "One day at a time," (from Alcoholics Anonymous) and "Be where your feet are," (from Anne Lamott). Still, the concept is so foreign to us that most of us only fleetingly experience the relief and energy available when we stop worrying about the future and take care of each moment as it comes. (For a good book on this subject, read *The Power of Now*, by Eckhart Tolle.)

I like what happens by combining Marilyn's two ideas. Imagine the effect if each of us began to live these simple guidelines. We'd be happier, because nothing nourishes us as well as real connection. We'd be more relaxed, because worrying about the future is draining. And who knows? This kind of real conversation, happening all over, could lead to remarkable outcomes.

Coaching Tips and Questions

- Within the next week, set up a time to get together with someone to whom you want to feel more connected.

- Be courageous and initiate conversations you've only imagined, speaking from the heart.

- Stop yourself whenever you realize you're focusing on the future. Ask instead, what's going on right now?

- Put mantras on your mirror or refrigerator to help remind you. Here are possibilities to get you started:
  - Be Brave
  - Live From Your Heart
  - Connect
  - One Day at a Time
  - Be Where Your Feet Are

5-4
DO SOMETHING DIFFERENT

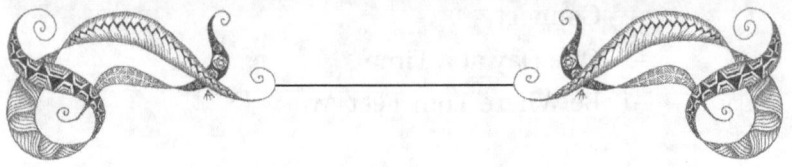

Insanity is doing the same thing over and over and expecting a different result.
— Albert Einstein

MAKING ONE SMALL CHANGE can help you get unstuck for two reasons.

> 1. CHANGE BEGETS CHANGE—THE SNOWBALL EFFECT
> Most of us find comfortable ways to operate in the world and stick with them even when they stop working. Changing one small, easy thing registers in the brain that change is possible. New neural circuits are laid. Interestingly, the change doesn't even have to be in the area identified as stuck.
>
> 2. WE OPERATE IN MANY SYSTEMS
> Our bodies are systems; our families are systems; and there are work systems, educational systems, and community systems. A change in one part of the system affects the whole system.
>
> Have you ever noticed when you have a toothache, your whole body feels out of sorts? The good news is that the system effect works the

same way with a positive change. It's been called a "benevolent spiral."

If you are stuck in any area:
- A personal or work relationship
- An ineffective team
- A recurring family argument
- A seemingly unsolvable problem
- A lifestyle that doesn't work for you

DO SOMETHING DIFFERENT—Change one, small thing.

Examples

- If you usually solve problems alone, ask a group to help.
- If you usually keep your feelings inside, talk about them.
- If you usually watch TV at night, take a walk instead.
- If you usually put your right shoe on first, start with your left.
- If your clutter distracts you from your work, move piles out of sight.

I recently asked a client how he accounted for the upbeat energy I heard in his voice. He told me that the previous evening he had told his wife in detail about how hard his work is right now. His usual way is to keep all his feelings inside, and, as his wife puts it, "crawl in a black hole." He made a conscious decision to do something different. The result was that his wife felt closer, he felt lighter, and, to his amazement, even the kids seemed relieved the next day.

Coaching Tips and Questions

- Identify an area in which you feel stuck in your life.
  - What one, small thing could you do differently in this area?
  - Do it!

5-5
SEASONS

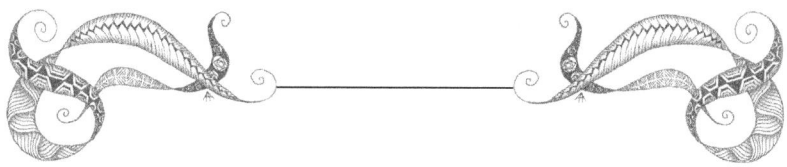

To everything there is a season, and a time to every purpose under the heaven.
— Ecclesiastes 3:1

WHEN CROCUSES COME UP, I know it is officially Spring! Although it is still cold, the back of winter is broken and I get itchy to be in the garden. In cultures where people live close to nature, the seasons are viewed as symbolic as well as playing an important role in daily life.

- *Spring*—the time of new ideas and creativity
- *Summer*—the time of partnership and holding greater purpose
- *Late Summer*—the time of harvest
- *Fall*—the time of accepting all that is and letting go
- *Winter*—the time of curiosity, wonder and deep quiet

There are seasons of life too: birth, childhood, puberty, early adulthood, middle age, late middle age, early old age, late old age, death. Each season seems to have its own joys and challenges. For example, my friend Susan calls the period when we have small children "the tired years." Dave told me recently he is having more fun at 60 than he's had for years. My mother asked, as she neared death, "How many steps are there to this dying stage of life?"

Perhaps the way we respond to the joys and challenges of each season is the thing that determines our quality of life. I loved learning recently of the Mid-Life Crisis Band, a group of men who formed a band instead of having affairs or buying red sports cars.

Although I love spring, winter is important in its own right. It's a time of inner happenings. Yoko Ono calls winter "the time of perseverance." I keep several bulbs in my basement all winter, cool, wrapped in breathable paper. I can't see what the bulbs are doing, but I know the quiet, dark time is important because when I plant the bulbs in the spring, they sprout and bloom exuberantly. I always hope my cold, quiet winter will have been as productive.

I love living where there are dramatic seasonal changes, because seasons remind me that nothing lasts too long. This helps me enjoy the loveliness and trust that what is less-than-lovely will pass, both in nature and in my life.

Coaching Tips and Questions

- What season are you in right now? What do you love about it? Write a page describing it.
- How do you change with the seasons? How can you use seasonal changes to stay flexible, open?
- How do the changing seasons work together to enhance your life?

- In which season are you least comfortable? Look at the description of the symbolism of seasons at the beginning of this essay, and ask yourself how to grow your comfort in that least comfortable season. It could grow your comfort in your whole life!
- Think about your relationships, projects, and organizations. What season is each in? How does that help you understand and improve them?

5-6

Small Systems

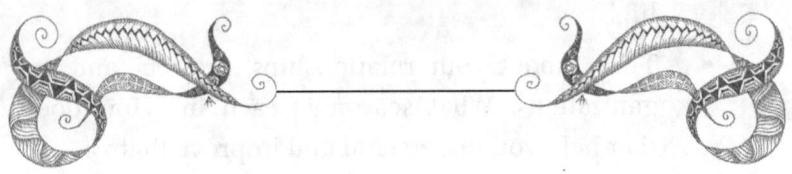

What we give we get back.
— C. Terry Warner

O NE MORNING I WAS STANDING IN LINE to buy corn at the Farmer's Market. A woman I didn't know was also waiting. She turned to me, smiling broadly, and said, "This makes me glad to be alive. Beautiful Saturday morning, fresh corn!" I looked at her, felt the connection, and smiled back, "Me too." As I walked back to my car, I realized that her smile and the connection had lifted me, setting me up for a great morning.

I often think of systems as big and complex, like the environment, the economy, or the inner workings of a company. But two people are also a system.

A system is defined as a group of interacting, interrelated, interdependent components that form a complex and unified whole. So my Farmer's Market friend and I qualify. We interacted; we were interrelated as standers in the corn line; and we were definitely interdependent. She influenced me, and I suspect that my response affected her back. In subtle, complex ways we connected and left smiling, uplifted.

These small systems created by two people are at the center of most of our lives. These are the systems that sustain and support us and the ones that trouble and vex us as well.

I once met a retired divorce lawyer. He told me this amazing story. He had been very successful, helping dissolve marriages, getting the most for his clients. After the lawyer retired, he began to wish he could help marriages repair instead of end, so he tried something new.

He still practiced some law, so when people asked if he would represent them in a divorce, the lawyer said, "I will. But I've learned there is a simple way to make sure the process goes well. You must do it before I'll accept your case. For the next month, treat your spouse with utmost kindness. Do it genuinely, because you want a good divorce. Come back in a month and I'll help you."

When the lawyer told me his story, he had tried this method on six couples. The results had been identical. At the end of a month, the complainant came back and thanked him for saving the marriage. What they'd discovered is what Terry Warner promises: What we give we get back.

Now I can hear someone saying, "You don't know so-and-so! I am consistently sweet to her and she treats me terribly." The truth is we can be sweet and outwardly cooperative, but if, underneath, we're judgmental and negative, that's what the other person will feel and respond to. How we see others is communicated subtly, and it affects how they see and respond to us.

If what Warner says is true, it is profound.

Here's the good news: If a small system is stuck, only one heart needs to shift. Eventually the other will not be responding to the same person. The way to make the change is to allow the truth of the other in, to allow ourselves to be influenced or touched by the other, which in itself touches the other. The small system reorganizes itself.

Coaching Tips and Questions

- How many small systems have you been part of today?
- Reflect carefully on this: Do you get what you give?
- How can you let the truth of the other in? Allow yourself to be touched by him or her?
- If there is tension in some of your systems, ask yourself:
  - How is it to be on the receiving end of me?
  - What if I'm wrong?

5-7

TRANSITIONS AND SYSTEMS

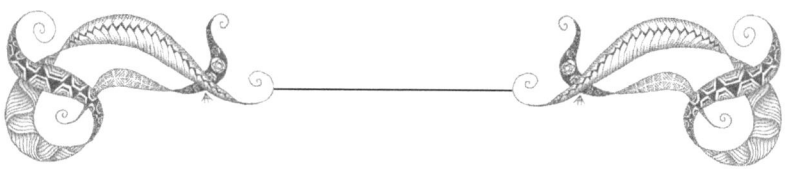

Life is one big transition.
— Willie Stargell

I REMEMBER RETURNING FROM A whirlwind trip to Wisconsin and California where I celebrated high school graduations with two grandchildren, Jessica and Mitchell. Major milestones! Both were looking forward to college and less regimentation. Their brothers and sisters couldn't imagine homes without them.

That fall, systems were surely disrupted—new patterns, alliances and habits emerged. The same thing happens in every family and organization when there is a transition.

My dad died one September, and our extended family had to figure out how to gather, celebrate, and spend time together without him. My friend Linsey and her husband had a baby, Amiel. This kind of transition is huge. One wonders how a critter so small can have such an impact—in feelings, daily habits, self-confidence. There are so many transitions going on every day:

- Individuals marry and become couples.
- Companies hire new presidents and executives.

- Couples get old and find themselves happy (or unhappy) to be helped to do things they used to do for themselves.
- People retire.

Transitions happen. They're a natural, inevitable part of life.

Every transition affects the systems that touch it. Research shows that people who struggle with transitions often have more anxiety, less satisfying relationships, and a poorer quality of life. Those who embrace change are less stressed and more resilient.

Coaching Tips and Questions

- What transitions can you embrace in your life now?
- What would it look and feel like to respond to the changes rather than resist them?
- What can you change in the next two days that will move you closer to embracing this transition?
- Take a careful look at all the other people affected by your transitions. How can you help them embrace the changes and thrive?

5-8
MAKE ROOM

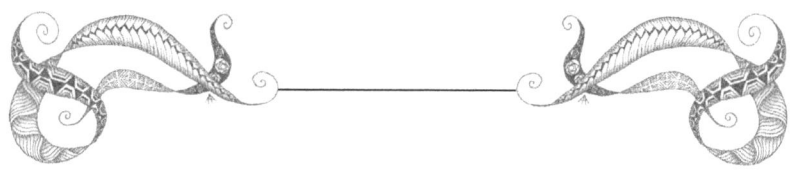

... after the first of the year ...
— nearly everyone

EVERY SO OFTEN WE ARRIVE AT JANUARY. This is the often mentioned "after the first of the year." If you really intend to start something new, you're likeliest to succeed if you first make room for it.

EXAMPLES

- Bob's team reluctantly closed an R&D project that had seemed exciting three years before. The setbacks had been relentless. Much time and money had been spent. The very next day they were presented with an opportunity that used much of what their failed research had taught them.
- Julia Cameron's book, *The Artist's Way*, includes an assignment of no reading for one week. This was torture for me. It was also magical. Without thinking about it, I hunted up my old wood carving tools. Without planning it, I started to dance.
- Steve stopped expecting his teen-aged daughter to be neat and helpful. What he discovered was that

she was bright and funny, and, when the pressure was off, sometimes even neat and helpful.

- Barbara finished her long, drawn-out house remodeling. Amazingly, as soon as that was done, her business took off.
- Angela gave away or threw away bags and boxes of long-accumulated possessions. The next week she met a wonderful man.
- One fall we cut down a 60 ft. tall, scraggly pine tree in our front garden. In the spring, a host of new plants and flowers came up, including some 15 ft. tall sunflowers, planted by birds. How long had they waited for light?

The connections are not always clear. What IS clear is that most of us do not have time, space, light, or energy for something new in our lives, even if we want it. Without some pruning, shifting, or clearing out on our part, we can expect more of the same.

Coaching Tips and Questions

- How might you let light into your life so dormant seeds can sprout?
- What unmet expectation might you drop, in order to see what IS there?
- What unfinished business can you complete, to make room for something fresh? When will you do it?

- What can you de-clutter? What mess can you erase, to open up a path for who knows what? Consider committing to 30 minutes of decluttering in the next week to get started.

5-9
IF YOU'RE STUCK, CLEAN A CLOSET

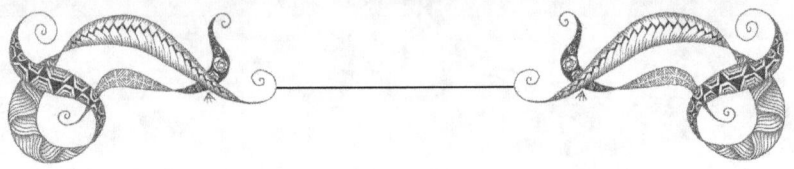

If you're feeling stuck in any area of your life, clean a closet or a drawer.
— Thomas Leonard

ONE DAY, I TOOK MY VACUUM CLEANER to the fix-it shop. It had stopped picking things up. The technician flipped the switch and said immediately, "Clogged inside." He disappeared to the back room for a short time and reappeared with the vacuum and a big smile. "The difference will be amazing," he said, "It's been getting clogged for a long time."

Here is a fact. When people who are overwhelmed or stuck in some way clean a closet or a drawer, they feel better. It's because we are each a system…and a clog in one part of the system bogs down the whole. Even out-of-sight, long ignored basement collections take up space inside of us and require invisible energy. We are much like my vacuum cleaner—getting clogged up over time.

When you unclog even a small part of the system, you will find it easier to complete things, start things, and move forward freely. Because time and space are connected, when you get more space, you will also get more time. And like the vacuum cleaner, you will be able to do more of what you were meant to do.

If you have trouble getting started, team up with a friend and help each other get into a purge and clean frenzy.

Coaching Tips and Questions

- Close your eyes and choose the first closet, drawer, corner of your desk, refrigerator, small section of the basement, or attic that comes to mind.
- Now purge and clean. The purge part is hardest. Here are guidelines: If you can't say "yes" to one of these questions, throw it out.
  - Do I love it?
  - Is it still alive for me?
- Target another area in a week.

5-10
Say No to Say Yes

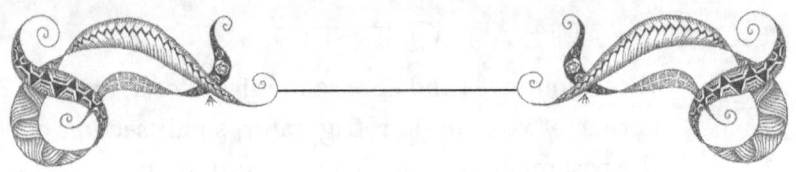

Our success comes from saying no to 1,000 things to make sure we don't get on the wrong track and try to do too much.
— Steve Jobs

"NO" MIGHT BE THE MOST IMPORTANT WORD in the English language. Whether and how you say "no" determines the very quality of your life. If you want to say "yes" to what really matters to you, you have to learn to say "no" with clarity, respect, and kindness.

There is always a trade off when you say "yes." Say, "yes" to one thing and you've automatically said "no" to anything else you might have done with that time. For instance, I agreed to give a talk for my business the day I got back from a family vacation. In doing so, I said "no" to a totally relaxed vacation. Recently I said "yes" to a big, delicious piece of cheesecake. In that moment, I said "no" to my earlier commitment to keep my calories down.

"No" is a simple word. It's also powerful. That's why it's hard. When you say it, you're afraid you'll hurt someone, disappoint them, or put them in a tight spot. And your concern is good. You're a generous spirit. You want to be helpful, not hurtful.

The only trouble is, every time you say "yes" to something you really don't have time for or interest in, the person you hurt, disappoint, or put in a tight spot is you.

Coach Cheryl Richardson says, "To get what you really, really want, you may have to give up what you really want." To help you decide when and how to say "no," it's helpful to get crystal clear on what you want to say "yes" to. Think about what matters most to you in your life.

Coaching Tips and Questions

- Think about your needs, your values, your goals, your dreams. Peel the onion. Reach down to your core. What is your deeper calling? What is true and right for you? What is the message from your heart and soul? The deeper you go into your "yes," the stronger your "no" will be.

- Write down three things that are "yeses" for you. They might be very specific or global. Here are some examples:
    - My family
    - Making enough money to pay the bills
    - Making lots of money
    - Being healthy
    - Helping people through my business
    - Making the world a better place
    - Loving fully and well

- Say "no"
    - Now every time someone asks you to volunteer for something or invites you to a party, instead of answering instantly, stop and think about it. Ask yourself if this activity lines up with your "yes." Consider what

you'll be saying "no" to if you say "yes" to this request.
- By going through this thought process, if you decide to say "no," it will be stronger and easier. You will be saying "no" to say "yes!"

5-11

HOLDING ON AND LETTING GO

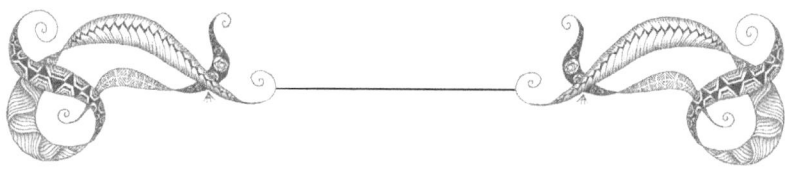

All the art of living lies in a fine mingling of letting go and holding on.
– Havelock Ellis

I READ THIS QUOTE FROM ELLIS and immediately flashed back to a vivid, teenage memory. Friends of my older brother took me water skiing for the first time. They gave me very little instruction, just, "There's nothing to it, but hold on for dear life." So I did. It was great fun for a while. Then I fell. And I continued to hold on for dear life, being dragged through the water until I thought I'd surely drown. Finally, my brother and his friends noticed I'd fallen and slowed the boat. They circled back to pick me up and said, "Next time hold on for dear life until you fall, and then let go for dear life." A good lesson.

There are many different parts of life in which, whether we realize it or not, we regularly make the choice to hold on or let go. Here are some:

- Opinions / assumptions / judgments
- Possessions
- Relationships
- Memories

- Habits

I shared the Ellis quote with friends and family and then surveyed them, asking "What would you like to hold on to and what would you like to let go of in this next year?" Here are the fascinating responses:

Hold on to:
- Loving relations with family—flowing all the time
- Rituals (not too stiff & rigid)
- Creativity
- People I can have meaningful conversations with on a variety of subjects
- Comforting daily rituals (tea, inspirational reading)
- Patience
- Noticing what's beautiful
- Health
- My inner self
- The roof over my head
- Wonderful memories of loved ones living and dead

Let go of:
- Superficiality
- Self-righteousness
- Worry
- Fighting changes that simply are
- Relationships where I can't have deep conversation
- Perfectionistic tendencies (would like to invite people over even if my house is cluttered)

- Blaming & complaining
- Martyrdom
- Clothes that still fit but I don't like them
- Physical facade
- Controlling ways
- Self aggrandizement
- Material things
- Being busy, busy, busy

Coaching Tips and Questions

- What would you like to hold on to?
- What would you like to let go of?
- Sit with these questions awhile and make your own list of each. Be honest. If the art of life truly is a mingling of holding on and letting go, it seems reasonable that our lives could be improved by making our choices thoughtfully.
- What will you let go of this week?

5-12
LIMITS TO GROWTH

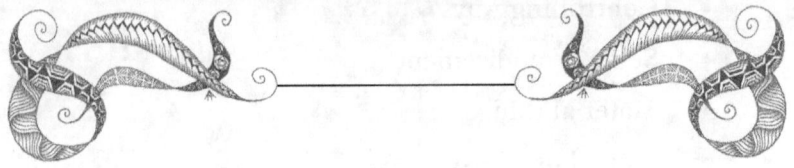

The truth is, we never grow without limits.
— Fifth Discipline Field Book

PART OF WHAT HAS MADE THE UNITED STATES GREAT is that we do not accept limits easily. After all, we have a long history of accomplishing the impossible. Combine these ingredients:

- Rugged individualism
- The sky's-the-limit, can-do attitude
- Capitalism

What do you get? A robust, competitive economic system of incredible creativity and productivity.

Ironically, the unwillingness to accept limits that makes our country great may also be our undoing. People cannot sustain 60 to 80 hour workweeks and thrive for long. We DO age. Death is natural. And a business cycle cannot escalate forever.

I submit that denial of natural limits is a mental model that helped build the context for the large-scale cheating that is showing up in United States businesses today. Without respect for natural limits, we get (among other things) what Greenspan called "infectious greed."

The upside of the current business crisis from a systems perspective is that the system has been disrupted. It will inevitably reorganize. If the reorganization acknowledges that growth has limits, we may create more sustainable systems.

Here are a few things that might help us on the path to creating more sustainable systems that acknowledge limits to growth.

- Practice proper selfishness—realize when enough is really enough and when our excesses impact others (and other systems).
- Change our mental model to think of ways that "bigger" might not be "better."
- Practice consciously accepting natural limitations. ("I did a lot today, even though it wasn't everything there was to do.")
- Challenge all "unnatural" boundaries (racism, sexism, etc.).
- When you find yourself working harder and harder to get the same result, consider that perhaps a limit is being approached. Change your focus to either loosening the limit or accepting that growth is slowing or stopping. (Working harder will only result in burnout and frustration.)
- Identify and work creatively with the limiting factors—usually goals, norms, or resources. (Don't confuse this with working creatively with the numbers.)
- Create win-win, cooperative ways to work rather than win-lose, competitive approaches.

- Insist that businesses broaden their understanding of "shareholders" to include employees, customers, suppliers, and communities, as well as stockholders.

Coaching Tips and Questions

- Choose two of the ideas listed above that resonate with you.
- What can you change to acknowledge the limits to growth in your own situation?
- When will you make the first change?

5-13
PERFECTING ENVIRONMENTS

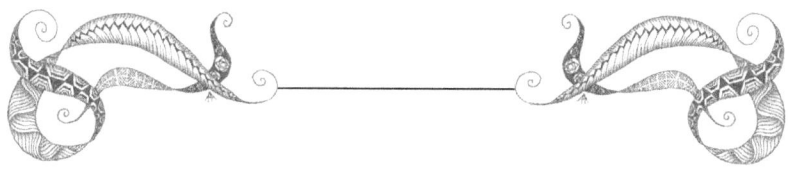

This place is scarrrreeeee!
– Uncle Bud on entering Costco
for the first time at age 77

IMAGINE REFRAMING ALL OF YOUR visions and goals, personal and professional, in terms of the environments required for them to happen. Then imagine setting to work creating those environments.

This is a refreshing systems approach. It's the reason a life coach might suggest you clean a closet when you're trying to solve a relationship problem. It acknowledges that changing one part of a system affects the others.

I once had a long talk with Thomas Leonard, the late founder of Coach U, about this possibility. He'd come up with key environments we all live in. The more you optimize all of the environments, we agreed, the better your life will be. Here are Thomas' key environments:

1. *Physical environment*—how you are affected by light, temperature, season, your living space
2. *Nature, out-of-doors*—the ways you are affected by and communicate with nature

3. *Ideas & information*—the things you read and listen to including media, friends, and family
4. *Feeling environment*—your habitual emotional undertone
5. *Energy environments*—the things that energize or drain you
6. *People environments*—the people with whom you choose to spend your time
7. *Time environments*—the times of day when you have more and less energy

Coaching Tips and Questions

- What small changes can you make in your living space that will make a big difference? What uncomfortable places can you avoid?
- What could you stop or start reading or listening to in order to increase positive ideas in your life?
- What negative emotion or habit are you willing to drop?
- When and where are you energized? Drained? What changes can you make to spend more time where you are energized and less where you are drained?
- Who's company do you enjoy? Who drags you down? Where can you find more people you enjoy?
- Which times of day work best for which activities in your life?
- Which of the seven environments need perfecting in your life?

- What will you do in the next week to move the process forward?

5-14
DEEPENING

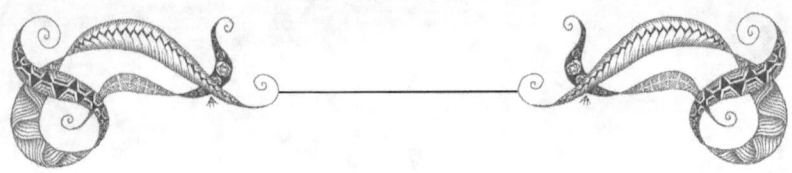

As knowledge increases, wonder deepens.
— Charles Morgan

I AM CONVINCED THAT AT SOME LEVEL WE ALL YEARN to deepen—our knowledge, our understanding, our acceptance, and our joy. We want deeper relationships, deeper faith, deeper fun, deeper calm, and deeper life.

Because each of us is a system, when we deepen any area of our lives, we feel energized all over.

EXAMPLES

KNOWLEDGE
- Go to the next level in some area where you are already knowledgeable. Read, study, and initiate conversations with other knowledgeable people. Ask a real expert in the field if you can pick her brain. (You'd be amazed how open many "experts" are to genuinely interested people.)

UNDERSTANDING
- Connect ideas, and then explain your insights to someone.
- Turn an insight into action.

RELATIONSHIPS
- Share a fear or a moment of vulnerability with a loved one.
- Have a deeper conversation with a neighbor.

ACCEPTANCE
- Figure out a new way to think about some annoying habit or tendency of a loved one so you find it endearing.
- Consciously stop trying to change something or someone you can't change.

PRACTICE
- Keep your focus on your breath as you exercise or do yoga.
- When you're introduced to someone, repeat the name, and ask how it is spelled. Write the name down so you'll remember it.
- Make conscious transitions between tasks, taking three deep breaths before moving on.

FAITH
- Read a sacred writing every day.
- Memorize a favorite prayer or inspiring quote.
- Add a period of quiet and stillness to your daily routine.

FUN
- You figure it out!

Deepening is maturing. Deepening takes courage because it often requires hoisting oneself out of a rut or running into a cement wall to slow down.

Coaching Tips and Questions

- Make a conscious decision to deepen one aspect of your life.
  - Notice any changes in your energy and aliveness.
  - Since energy and aliveness are often contagious, notice if your deepening has a positive effect on others.
- Repeat the above steps on another aspect of your life.

Chapter 6

Giving Back

GIVING BACK

We make a living by what we get. We make a life by what we give.

– Winston Churchill

CHURCHILL'S WORDS SAY IT ALL. To thrive, we must give back. In fact, life is full, rich, rewarding, satisfying, and exciting to the extent that we give back. Giving means we are involved with people and projects, engaged with others, passing along our wisdom, sharing our talents, and giving whatever we have to give.

My friend Eunice Summer raised her children using what she called "The Entertainment Theory of Childrearing." This theory required that she provide for their basic needs, and they were obliged in return to entertain her: to be funny, to play, and to help her stay young. Her theory actually worked! Whenever I was wearing childrearing too heavily, I found Eunice's perspective inspiring.

Giving back may be the greatest of all pleasures. When a person says she just wants to be happy, I often think, "Then give more." She should not give out of obedience or because she "should," but for the pure joy of giving, of contributing, of being part of the great and strange universe as it turns. For many, many years, whenever I have felt a little tight on money, I give money to charity. I'm not sure how it works, but it seems to loosen something up in me and in the universe. I feel better, and the tightness passes.

Some young people I know adopted a family last Christmas. They learned all about the ages of the kids and the kinds of things they liked. The young people went shopping, using their own money, at Target and at the Thrift Shop. They were thoughtful about it. When the time came to deliver the gifts, they took them to the family. A 13-year-old helped a 9-year-old ride a new bike. Later he told me, "That was the best part of my Christmas! That kid was thrilled to have a bike. And he really needed my help to ride it. I can't believe how good that felt. I want to do that every year."

When a person can give back in a generous spirit, in however large or small a way, the reward is automatic, it is built in. We feel connected, part of the whole. Consider the essays in this section with your own habits around giving in mind. Giving to others, in the many creative ways possible, will enrich your own life exponentially.

6-1

PURPOSE

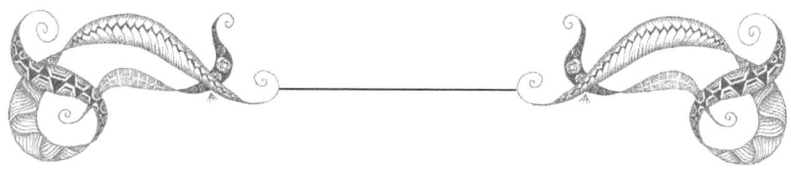

Purpose is what gives life a meaning.
— Charles Perkhurst

TO LIVE A LIFE ON PURPOSE MEANS we use our natural gifts and talents, usually in a way that ripples out to benefit a larger world. If you have found yourself wanting more meaning in your life or asking, "Is this all there is?" you are probably yearning to uncover your purpose.

Fortunately, we all seem to be born with a purpose, so we don't have to create it. We just have to uncover ours. Purpose is not a goal. It is a direction, and we never "arrive"—we just know we are "on" or "off" purpose. We feel this in our bones. Purpose gets us up in the morning and sustains our energy.

Many, maybe even most, of us want to live a meaningful life, a life filled with purpose, but we put off finding the time and making the effort to uncover our purpose. We get distracted, thinking that material success will give us meaning, fulfillment, and a sense of who we are. It seldom does. When we uncover our purpose, we get a larger vision of ourselves and a clearer sense of how we fit in the world. Purpose brings out the best in us and makes difficulties easier.

Examples

Leon Eakes

My dad, Leon Eakes, is a wonderful example of how living on purpose can be expressed throughout life. A strong purpose in his life is to continually improve himself and others through learning and education. He worked his way through college with many small, entrepreneurial jobs. As a Naval officer in WWII, he encouraged the men on his ship to use the GI bill and go to college. Many did.

Just last year Dad received a letter from one of those men, thanking him for a wonderful life. Before my dad's influence, this man had never considered going to college. When the man wrote to express his thanks, he'd just retired from a 50+-year career as an engineer.

When my siblings and I were growing up, our going to college was assumed and supported. When various of our friends had financial difficulty continuing in school, my dad quietly made loans available. Many people lived with my parents while going to school.

My dad, a businessperson, subscribed to and read the first of the business books, always learning, improving himself, and passing on his wisdom. At 94, my dad continues to make a generous contribution to a scholarship fund at the University of Pacific each year. And at Oak Creek, his assisted living residence, he is an active cheerleader for many of the aides. He encourages them to become registered nurses or therapists of some kind, to learn more and use their gifts and talents to the fullest. I suspect this strong purpose of my dad's has something to do with his remaining mentally sharp!

ALISON RICH

Artist Alison Rich expresses her purpose through painting. Rich's glorious portraits breathe. When I first saw them, I was nearly speechless. The eyes seem to move and change in the light. The nuances of color on faces make the people 3-dimensional. I asked Rich how she makes this magic with watercolors.

She described her technique: Rich meets the person, photographs the subject repeatedly from various angles, in different environments. At that initial meeting, she mixes colors for the face. Sometimes it takes 30 pigments. She sketches the person. Then the portrait begins.

Rich looked radiant as she described this process, concluding simply, "I've come to know my purpose in life is to bring people's spirits to life in paintings."

George Bernard Shaw had it right when he said, "This is the true joy in life—the being used for a purpose recognized by yourself as a mighty one."

COACHING TIPS AND QUESTIONS

- In writing, describe two or three times in your life when you did something that left you feeling deeply fulfilled or satisfied.

- Reread what you've written, asking, "What are the similarities? What themes repeat? How might what I've written give clues to my purpose?"
- Get help in discovering your purpose by reading one of these books:
  - *Liberating Greatness, the Whole Brain Guide to an Extraordinary Life*, by Hal Williamson and Sharon Eakes
  - *Now What? 90 Days to a New Life Direction*, by Laura Berman Fortgang

6-2

GIFTS FROM THE HEART

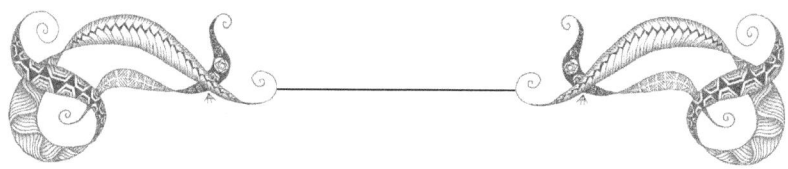

The greatest gift is a portion of thyself.
— Ralph Waldo Emerson

HERE'S AN ADVENTURE that actually happened to my grandpa when he was a teenager, before the invention of the automobile. Grandpa called it "A Real Halloween Ghost Story." Grandpa and some friends decided to play a Halloween prank on their favorite teacher. Mr. Barker's carriage was parked in front of his house, without the horses. The boys rolled it into the teacher's garage. They hoped he'd think a ghost moved it. But in the end, they were the ones who were startled. Just as they got the carriage parked, a deep voice said, "Thank you, boys." It scared them to death! Turns out Mr. Barker was sitting in the carriage all the time!

I know that story because my grandfather wrote it down, along with a couple of others, and gave it to me one Christmas. It was a gift from his heart that I treasure.

Christmas is always just around the corner! This year, consider giving gifts that cost less and say more: gifts from the heart. These are not the gifts you are likely to see on TV or those that populate the catalogs flooding our homes at holiday time.

Sometimes gifts from the heart take a little time and imagination. If you start now, though, one of the joys you'll experience is that gifts from the heart enrich the giver. With a little thought, you can come up with perfect gift ideas for the big and little people about whom you really care. Here are some ideas.

A GIFT OF LOVE
- Write a story from your life—an adventure, a funny experience, or a time you overcame a difficulty. Give the story to your children or grandchildren.
- Write a letter or a poem to a loved one, including all the reasons you love him or her.

GIFTS OF TIME
- Give a coupon for a special activity—a candlelight dinner, a massage, a trip to the zoo. (One of my favorite presents from my son when he was little was a coupon for a 10-minute foot massage.)
- Plan a monthly lunch date with a seldom-seen relative or friend.
- Give a coupon for several hours or a weekend of babysitting.
- Give a coupon to wash someone's car or house windows.
- Offer a particular talent such as photography, gardening, financial planning, hairstyling, or fixing things.

HOMEMADE GIFTS
- Make audio or video interviews of parents, grandparents, aunts, and uncles. You can ask them to discuss their memories of the recipient, your fami-

ly's history, their favorite jokes, whatever! You can even put the interviews on YouTube.

- Make a book from photos. Many photo websites (like www.ShutterFly.com) make it easy and affordable to make a book of photos.

GIFTS OF EXPERIENCE
- Offer to teach the recipient a skill you possess, such as canning tomatoes, making salsa, knitting, woodcarving, fishing, speaking French, or making origami cranes.

GIFTS OF CHARITY
- Donate to a cause in the name of the recipient.
- Sponsor a child refugee, support a homeless shelter, or protect an acre of rainforest.
- Give a flock of chicks, a goat, or part of a pig to an impoverished family. Heifer International, www.Heifer.org, is one of my favorite unusual gift sites.

Coaching Tips and Questions

- Plan some gifts from the heart for people in your life. These gifts work for Hanukkah, birthdays, and Ayyám-i-Há as well as Christmas!

6-3

Real Help

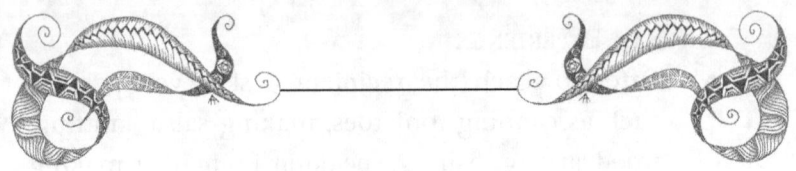

When a person is down in the world, an ounce of help is better than a pound of preaching.
— Edward G. Bulwer-Lytton

WHEN I WAS ABOUT TO MOVE from an apartment to a house, a woman I hardly knew, who lived down the hall, left a message under my door saying, "If you need packing help, I'm a helluva packer." I was happy to accept her offer, because I happen to be a terrible packer.

Marge, a retired army nurse, arrived at my door the next night. When she looked at my packed boxes, she said, "Oh, dear. Worse than I thought."

She plunged in unpacking and repacking what I'd started, cutting the number of boxes I needed in half! Marge was direct and no-nonsense and came back for three nights, teaching me as we went, until we were done. I felt the whole time that she had sensed my great need and responded with real help.

I thought of Marge when my friend Kathy suggested "Real Help" would be a great topic for a "Fresh Views." Real help is very different from the common, "Let me know what

I can do to help," that many of us offer. Real help assesses the situation and responds to the heart of the need.

As a therapist, Kathy once went to her boss feeling confused and overwhelmed. She was feeling desperate and had no idea how to get out of that chaotic place. After hearing Kathy's unsorted-out problem, her boss asked, "What would relieve you the most?" Kathy thought a bit and then said one thing really bogging her down was a bunch of late discharge summaries. Her boss simply said, "Give them to me and I'll do them."

Years later, as Kathy remembers this event, vivid feeling remains. She told me it was hard to convey in words the surprise and relief she felt when her boss knew what Kathy needed more than she did. She's not sure what she had expected—maybe a lecture on better time management, which would have added to her burden. Kathy was clear: "I want to say how big this was for me. It actually changed me forever and taught me life can surely change on a dime."

Real help is usually concrete. It can include introducing just the right person or resource, bringing soup, or offering help with packing, to mention just a few possibilities.

Examples

- I lamented to my friend Peg that Rosa, the woman caring for my elderly uncle, speaks only Spanish. In spite of having taken high school Spanish, I speak very little. Spanish-speaking family members have helped, but aren't always available. Peg said, "There are so many services available these days. Look online. I'm sure you'll find a translation service." And I did! It was so easy, but the idea had never occurred to me. I cannot tell you how

- this has helped me! I can now call Rosa 24 hours/day with the support of a translator.
- Anna told me about her friend Wendy, who is going through much loss and suffering about her son-in-law who is battling cancer. The prognosis is dire. Wendy has been active in his care and doing a million other things. She mentioned to Anna that her watch had stopped working. Anna brought her one of her watches until Wendy could get the "time" to get hers fixed. Real help.
- When my second husband Gene died, I wanted to talk about him more than anyone wanted to hear. Sensing my need, my friend Tina invited me to talk about Gene to my heart's content. What a wonderful, welcome invitation. I talked about him for hours. She listened intently. It was an important part of my grieving.

Real help responds precisely to someone's need. It requires that the helper be present, tuned in, willing to respond, and courageous enough to do or say the odd thing to fill that need.

To be on the receiving end of real help is to be deeply touched, to feel the goodness of humankind, to be lifted!

Coaching Tips and Questions

- When have you received real help? Think about what it was, how it felt.
- What obstacles keep you from offering real help? For example, do you feel intrusive? Do you feel your help might be rejected?

- What obstacles keep you from asking for and/or accepting real help?
- Where in your life do you feel called to offer real help now?

6-4
INITIATIVE

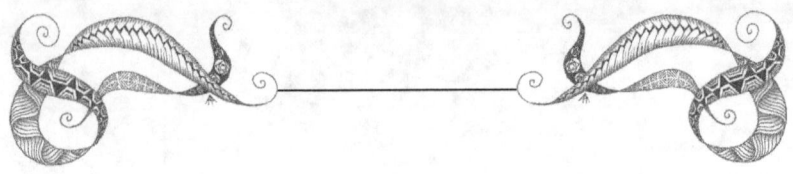

Initiative is doing the right thing without being told.

– Victor Hugo

I'VE BEEN THINKING ABOUT "INITIATIVE." Recently I joined the YMCA. Since I tend to get sluggish about exercise, I am proud of myself. I told a friend I'd "taken the initiative" for my health. (I've worked out 5 times, lifted 3,000 pounds today, and feel terrific! Endorphins are for real.)

The woman who signed me up at the Y also took initiative. Barbara was new at the information desk, and she'd never signed up a new member—it isn't part of her job. Yet she saw there was a line and said, "I think I can help you." In the process, she had to run and ask a couple of questions, but she did it just fine and I was grateful not to wait.

Robert Kelley, a Carnegie Mellon University Professor, did a landmark study of what it takes to be a star at work called *How To Be A Star At Work*. "Demonstrating initiative" proved to be the most powerful skill that differentiated the super productive, star worker from the intelligent, average worker. Taking initiative doesn't mean just doing your job well. It means willingly moving out of your job description spheres to fill gaps.

Dr. Kelley's research shows that within two years on a job, star performers begin to look for systemic problems to tackle. This higher-level systems perspective enables them to take initiatives which solve a whole set of similar problems throughout an entire system.

Putting his research into practice, Dr. Kelley and colleagues began to teach the "star" strategies. They found that people could be taught to take more initiative but that it required a shift of mind. People had to stop complaining about their jobs and begin looking for ways to take initiative.

Coaching Tips and Questions

- Reflect on your current attitude: How much of your time and energy are you spending complaining vs. taking initiative to make things better?
- If you want to be a star at work, begin to take initiative. Do the right thing without being told.
- Take some initiative that improves your life—join the Y, clean your basement, invite friends over.

6-5
JEN RATIO

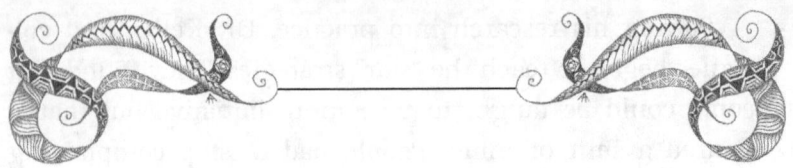

Jen ratio is a simple but powerful way of looking upon the relative balance of good and uplifting versus bad and cynical in life.
– Dacher Keltner

JEN IS THE CENTRAL IDEA IN THE TEACHINGS of Confucius. It refers to a complex mixture of kindness, humanity, and respect that transpires between people. Simply put, the *jen* ratio is the relationship of positive emotions like compassion, gratitude and sympathy to negative emotions like anger, cynicism, contempt. The *jen* ratio can be measured in an individual, a family, a neighborhood, a company, a city, or a nation. High *jen* ratios, whether in an individual or an organization, result in people being happier, living lives that are more meaningful.

In his book *Born to be Good*, Dacher Keltner describes the scientific studies now being done at the University of California, Berkeley's Greater Good Science Center, "an interdisciplinary research center devoted to the scientific understanding of happy and compassionate individuals, strong social bonds, and altruistic behavior." (Check out *Greater Good* magazine online, which carries stories of this research.)

This research is giving credence to a view in stark contrast to the notion that self-interest is what drives and satisfies us. The big news discovery is that what often makes us happiest is bringing the good in others to completion. This is a profound notion—that not only are we happiest when we focus on others, but when we're in service to them.

This research is cross-cultural, even cross-species. "The right kind of smile brings the good in others to completion. It is one of the first acts of *jen* in primate evolution."

I find myself thinking about this *jen* ratio in all kinds of practical ways. There are people I know who definitely have a high *jen* ratio—they are responsive to others and upbeat. There are others with a low *jen* ratio. These people tend to be negative and stuck. Similarly, I "feel" the ambience when I go into a store or restaurant. In these terms, the businesses with a high *jen* ratio are welcoming, inviting me to have a good experience.

The notion of the *jen* ratio gives new meaning to my profession as a coach. For the last 16 years, I have felt so lucky to be in this business. What a delight it is to help others become their best selves, move toward whatever feels like completion for them. How blessed I am to have a built-in *jen*-raising job!

In a serious illness, I realized that allowing friends to be helpful to me is a gift to them (instead of being fiercely independent). I now give people the opportunity to raise their *jen* ratios.

I also like to think of the big ramifications of high *jen* ratios. According to Keltner, "High *jen* ratios promote a society's economic and ethical progress. *Jen* becomes viral through behaviors that spread goodness from one individual to the next, thus setting in motion reinforcing, reciprocal cooperation." Think of how the world could be changed just by raising our *jen* ratios!

Coaching Tips and Questions

- What is your *jen* ratio? (Think of emotions that describe you best. Put the positive ones in the numerator and the negative in the denominator. Which is stronger?)
- How does your *jen* ratio differ at home and at work?
- What happens when you become aware of *jen* ratios all around you?
- How might you raise your *jen* ratio?
- How might you help others raise theirs?

6-6
LIFE—A WORK OF ART

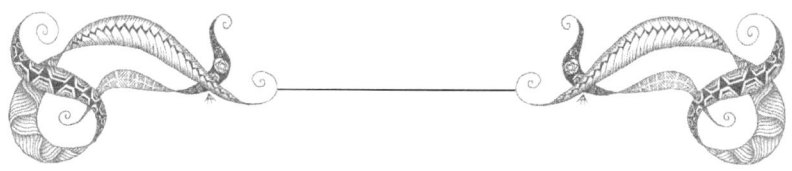

Beholding the work of art they wrought by clinging to life, I am flooded with a feeling like joy, deepened by astonishment that human beings were capable of such a creation.

– David Roberts

THE QUOTE ABOVE IS THE LAST SENTENCE in David Roberts' book, *Four Against the Arctic, Shipwrecked for Six Years at the Top of the World*. It details the amazing story of four Russian men who survived for six years in the Arctic, beginning in 1743.

A reader can be inspired by such a story, identify with parts of it, and glean useful lessons from it. Roberts suggests instead that we take a fresh view: seeing their survival as a work of art, which delights, astonishes, and inspires us!

This suggestion prompted me to think about the usual year-end reviews many of us do—personally and in our companies. We detail accomplishments, joys, disappointments, unfinished projects, etc. This can be very useful.

How about doing it differently this year—viewing your year as a work of art?

Coaching Tips and Questions

Ask yourself a few questions to flesh out the art:

- Is your work of art a painting? A sculpture? A symphony? A novel? A tapestry?
- Is it colorful or muted?
- Is it big, medium-sized, or small?
- Where is the energy?
- Where are the shadows?
- How does your art incorporate the highs and lows of the year?
- How does it look ahead?
- How has it given back—to family, friends, community, company, and future generations?
- What difference would it make, in your life or your company, if you lived every day conscious of the work of art you were creating?

6~7
CONTRIBUTION

When you cease to make a contribution, you begin to die.

– Eleanor Roosevelt

I THINK A LOT ABOUT CONTRIBUTING. My favorite coaching clients are bright, gifted people who want to make big contributions. A person can contribute in so many ways—by being a thoughtful leader, a caring parent, a helpful neighbor. Contributions can come in various forms: time, ideas, support, energy, and money, to name a few.

The best story I've heard lately about making a contribution comes from Nyan Pendyala, age 9. He and his 6-year-old sister Lehka started the Kids for Sight Project. They're working with ORBIS International, a charity that has been helping prevent blindness worldwide for 25 years. I interviewed Nyan for this essay, asking first how he got involved in this project.

"Well," he said, "I stopped my dad when he was flipping through a newsletter from ORBIS International and I saw a picture of Ronald McDonald. I wanted to know what Ronald McDonald was doing there. I found out he was helping keep kids from becoming blind by building an eye hospital in New Delhi. I said, 'I should help with that!'"

"Try this," Nyan said to me. "Close your eyes for 20 seconds. How does it feel? Scary? That's how a blind kid feels. I really wanted to help, so I asked my friends to donate to ORBIS instead of bringing presents to my birthday party. My dad and I called ORBIS and told them how I'd raised money for them. Because I was the first kid they knew of to raise money at a birthday party, they invited me to visit them. Their office is in New York City so we went there, and they helped me choose the place for my donation: building a pediatric eye care center and training facility in Chennai, a poor town where my dad was born and my grandparents still live."

To my question about what he's done since then to raise money, Nyan said, "The ORBIS people put us on their website. We made postcards and I've given them to all my family and friends and my parents' friends. I gave a speech to 80 people and it was easy. Now I'm trying to find connectors, people with lots of friends. If I can inspire connectors, they will inspire lots of other people and I can help the kids faster. Because you know what? If you can catch an eye problem early, the kid doesn't get blind."

As I talked with Nyan, I was struck by how animated he was, how happy. I asked him how this project made him feel. "Really good!" was his intense response.

A funny irony came to me. We all want our children to be happy. Maybe more happiness would result if we shifted from asking, "What can I give my child that will make him happy?" to asking, "How can I inspire her to contribute?" I'm a connector for Nyan.

Coaching Tips and Questions

- How do you contribute? (time, ideas, support, energy, money, prayers)
- With each person in your life, whether a family member or someone you meet for the first time, ask yourself, "How can I contribute to this person?"
- How might you give back by contributing to your community? (highway clean-up, block watch, harvesting leftovers in the fields for a community food bank?)
- Is there a big cause, like Nyan's, for which you'd like to raise awareness and money? How will you start? When?

Conclusion:

Resilient Living

RESILIENT LIVING

The greatest glory in living lies not in never falling, but in rising every time we fall.

– Nelson Mandela

This book has offered many seemingly different ideas and insights—improving both mind and body, seeing connections everywhere, giving back—but what ties them all together is *resilience*. My hope for you is that you will live a resilient life. That is why I want to end this book by sharing my thoughts about what such a life might look like.

Resilient living is a state of well-being that continues, in spite of life's inevitable difficulties. It is more than toughing it out. It's actually thriving because of our ups and downs, by learning from them. It is purposefully taking on challenges to strengthen ourselves. Resilient people learn to connect well with others, since we are always in relationships of one kind or another. A resilient person has a sense of perspective and can always find something for which to be grateful. Every essay in this book is about becoming more resilient.

Resilience includes how we think about things—even how we see them. Is the glass half-full, or half-empty? It is about learning and getting stronger and relaxing into ourselves. It is about asking for help and accepting help offered. Resilient people know and care for themselves in many ways.

Resilient living is about being compassionate toward others—even those who rub us wrong—and seeing their humanity. It is about believing that in some way things will work out—that meaning will come even if it isn't clear at first. Resilience is about creativity in solving problems and in living, including art in those solutions in all its beautiful forms—paintings, stories, music, theater. It is about responding to life with all our parts.

Resilience is about developing and using our sense of humor: to bear things, to laugh at ourselves, to stay upbeat. It is about honoring the physical body so it stays energized—eating healthily, exercising, giving the body breaks, and downtime. Resilience is the result of being in the habit of generosity—with time, money, energy, thoughts—giving back—to the people in our lives, the communities we live in, and the causes we believe in.

Resilient living requires dropping some old ways:
- Blame, self-righteousness, victimhood, helplessness, powerlessness, bullying, gossiping
- Seeing things always in a negative light
- Sitting on the couch overeating
- Believing happiness can be bought
- Using physical strength or violence to solve problems

Each of these diminishes resilience.

Yet cultivating resilience requires that we experience challenges, that we do some things that are hard for us. Ironically, we need our struggles. They strengthen us. Without them, how do we know what we're capable of? In this light, a parent's natural desire to protect her child from pain and difficulty can be misguided. Our children also need their struggles.

Our struggles may be huge and dramatic—loss of a loved one or a pet, a serious illness, a natural disaster. Most struggles are smaller by comparison, but no less important in terms of building resilience: making it through a semester of school with a teacher we find difficult, forgiving what feels like a betrayal, surviving the break-up of a relationship, or getting through a really hard day at work.

Like all people, my own life is an ongoing story about how resilience builds. Here are two very different examples. The first is a story about a hard day at work.

It was a Saturday, Family Day, at a residential drug and alcohol addiction treatment center in the early 1970's. There were over 100 patients and many family members visiting. I was 30 years old, a relatively new therapist, and I was in charge. There were also a receptionist and 2 nurses on duty. We had completed the educational part of the day, when one patient started banging his head on the floor. He wouldn't stop. I was trying to figure out what to do when someone came to inform me that another patient had taken a visitor's baby, ostensibly to protect her from "the sniper on the roof." Inspection showed no sniper on the roof. Our regular psychiatrist was a rabbi as well, and not on duty on Saturdays. Somehow, I got through that day. The head banger's family came for him. With help from other patients, the baby was coaxed from the arms of the hallucinating patient. Arrangements were made with a back-up psychiatrist, also difficult to find, to transfer that man for mental health treatment.

It was the worst workday of my life. AND YET, so much good came from it. I lobbied successfully for more staffing on the weekends. We got to know the back-up psychiatrist. We learned to screen patients better for mental illness. And no stressful day ever seemed very difficult after that. My resilience went up a notch that day.

The second example is about choosing to take on challenges, and practicing until they get easier.

Two mornings a week I do a series of 12 exercises called High-Intensity Circuit Training Using Body Weight. They're slightly beyond my comfort zone. You're supposed to repeat each movement 30 times. With each movement I get to 15 and think, "Well, I'm half-way done." At 20, I think, "Yeah, only 10 to go." And so I get through them. The exercises take me 8 minutes to do and every part of me gets stronger in the process: my body, my spirit, my resolve, my sense of myself as a strong, healthy woman.

The essays in this book are all about learning from life's ups and downs, and increasing one's capacity to live well. I hope that reading them, answering some of the coaching questions and trying some of the coaching tips, has benefitted you in tangible ways, growing your resilience.

Ultimately, resilient living is about expanding the human spirit, actualizing the potential waiting to be developed in each of us. May your spirit soar!

ACKNOWLEDGEMENTS

I AM ENORMOUSLY GRATEFUL TO MY PARENTS, Leon and Weedie Eakes, who modeled resilient living. They also loved me unconditionally for 60+ years. The only thing to do with such a gift is to pass it on.

I am profoundly thankful to Bahá'u'lláh, founder of the Bahá'í Faith, and to my vibrant Pittsburgh Bahá'í community for continued guidance, inspiration, and support.

To my family, thank you for being there for me in so many ways. My children, stepchildren, grandchildren, and great-grandchildren are the motivation for publishing this book. I hope you can find encouragement, a "fresh view," in these pages even after I've gone on to another world.

My late husband Hal was often my first reader, and his suggestions and support were invaluable.

I cannot find words strong enough to describe how important my friends are to me. Day in and day out, they sustain me. They have often been my inspiration for "Fresh Views" topics, and friends almost always help me think my essays through. Special thanks to Sallie, Stephanie, Jan, Dona, Maria, and Astrid. Gratitude to Dennis Daley, Marnie Haines, and Ginny Wiley who encouraged me for more than 10 years to gather and publish these essays. Thank you, thank you, all for your support!

A special heartfelt acknowledgement to those dear friends who shepherded this volume into being: Peg Stewart, publisher of the *Green Tree Times;* Bill Weil, who coached me through the first organizing steps; Bonnie Budzowski, who provided valuable edits and coached me through the last; Rick Budzowski who played with me to get the formatting just right; Barbara Curry, who created the cover, happily offering one after another until I LOVED it; and Aleta

Ahktar, who created the Zendoodles to introduce the chapters and essays.

Last, but certainly not least—I want to thank my responsive readers. Your interest keeps me writing. Thank you from the bottom of my heart!

I continue to write "Fresh Views" each month, so if you'd like to receive them, go to www.hopellc.com and subscribe.

ABOUT THE AUTHOR

Sharon's energy has always been directed toward helping people live balanced, productive, joyful lives. She began her career by obtaining a master's degree in psychology. Sharon went on to be a therapist for many years and then a healthcare executive for twenty years. She leveraged the skills and experiences from those early roles to develop an executive coaching practice. As a Board Certified Coach, she continues to help leaders make meaningful contributions to their organizations and the world. She currently coaches individuals and couples as well. Since 2009, Sharon has been a trainer for the Arbinger Institute. She co-leads the acclaimed master coaching program—The Choice in Coaching.

Sharon continues to publish "Fresh Views" and "Musings" each month. She has presented at many national conferences, and has been an invited guest on TV and radio shows.

Random pieces of information about Sharon that tell more of the whole story:

- Sharon was born and raised in Stockton, California.
- Sharon was (and still is) called Pam by her family and friends in California.
- Sharon's mom and dad were happily married for 69 years! What a model. Her dad was outgoing and social, her mom shy and quiet. They leaned into each other's strengths and created magic.
- Although Sharon has lots of formal training, she feels her best training for the work she does came from working every summer at Stockton Silver Lake Family Camp in the High Sierras. First she was a crew member, then the Program Director.

There she not only removed mouse nests full of baby mice from drawers in tents, but got people singing together around the campfire and convinced grown men to be in silly skits.

- At age 19, after two years of college, Sharon married her high school sweetheart, Roger Mitchell.
- After their junior year in college, Sharon and Roger took a break from school with the intention of building a boat and sailing around the world. Getting pregnant changed the plan, so they built a cabin in the woods in Inverness-by-the-Sea, California.
- Baby Lisa was born in 1965. They all lived in that cabin in the woods for a year, without electricity or running water in the house.
- When Sharon got pregnant with Gordon, she and Roger built a second cabin in the woods and added running water (even a primitive, flushing toilet) inside!
- One month before Gordon was born, Sharon graduated from UC Davis, cum laude, with a major in English and a minor in psychology.
- Sharon taught piano and pre-school music for eight years.
- Sharon and Roger sold the cabins in the woods to her best friend, and moved to Pittsburgh, PA, to attend graduate school at Duquesne University, where they both majored in Existential Phenomenological Psychology. Lisa was 3 and Gordon was 1 when they started. Sharon earned a master's degree in psychology in 1970 and taught psychology at Duquesne in 1971.

- Sharon and Roger divorced in 1971. She dropped out of the Ph.D. program.

- For two years that were difficult for all concerned, the children lived with Roger and his new wife, Kay, and saw Sharon on the weekends and summers.

- The children returned to live with Sharon. Roger completed his degree and moved back to California. Sharon stayed in Pennsylvania, which had become her true home.

- Sharon was a single parent for many years. The kids visited their dad in the summer.

- Sharon and her two brothers (Lon and Jon) and sister (Wendy) all got divorced at least once. Apparently, each was aiming to replicate the magic of their parents. Eventually all succeeded.

- Sharon worked first as a therapist and then as the Vice President of Treatment Programs at Gateway Rehabilitation Center, for 25 years. She helped grow Gateway from a single site and level of care, to 10 sites in 6 counties, with many levels of care. She loved working with drug and alcohol addicts.

- Sharon fell in love with Gene Curley, who was an internist. They were a couple for 18 years, marrying after Lisa and Gordon were in college. Gene was her soulmate. They had a magical marriage. He died suddenly in 1992.

- Sharon served on the Pennsylvania Task Force on Women and Addiction for many years, and founded the Regional Task Force on Women and Addiction in Allegheny County.

- After 4 years as a widow, Sharon left Gateway to marry Hal Williamson in 1996. They were happily married for nearly 16 years. In 2006, they wrote a book together, *Liberating Greatness, the Whole Brain Guide to an Extraordinary Life*.

- Sharon has always been drawn to the spiritual side of life. Both of her grandfathers were protestant ministers, and she was active in the Methodist church as a kid. However, when she was 16, the accusation that her beloved pastor was a Communist became an issue. He was tried in front of the House Un-American Activities Committee and found innocent. However, in those fear-infested times, the hype tore the church apart. People who had been best friends stopped speaking to each other. Sharon was disillusioned that the people in the church couldn't find in the religion any way to resolve their differences. She left organized religion for 40+ years. For the years that she worked in drug and alcohol treatment, the principles of Alcoholics Anonymous served her as guidance.

- In 2002, Sharon and Hal joined the Bahá'í Faith. She remains an active and committed member of the vibrant Pittsburgh Bahá'í community. She gets strength and inspiration from her Faith and friends there.

- For 10 years, Sharon served as the chair of the Board of Directors of Pegasus Communications, a Systems Thinking publishing house and conference company.

- In 2003, Hal was diagnosed with cone dystrophy. He became legally blind. Adding what he knew

- about brain science to his upbeat attitude and remarkable discipline, he amazed doctors by regaining much of his sight 3 years later.

- Toward the end of his life, Hal became frail and developed dementia. Sharon's caregiving was made easier because he grew increasingly sweet and patient. He died following a fall in 2012.

- Sharon is the survivor of a rare and aggressive form of endometrial cancer. She had surgery, chemotherapy, and radiation in 2012.

- Sharon stays fit and practices Qigong daily. Her qigong master is Mingtong Gu, called the "laughing guru."

- In 2014, Sharon and her daughter Lisa went on a walking tour of Ireland. It was a dream trip! They walked 70 miles. She plans a walking tour of Iceland with her son Gordon in 2015.

- In early 2015, Sharon and her colleague Nancy Smyth co-authored a book titled *Chocolate or Lunch, How Choice Impacts Relationships.*

- Sharon has 2 children, 4 stepchildren, 14 grandchildren, and 4 great-grandchildren. She loves them to pieces!

- Sharon is a whittler, watercolor painter, and Zendoodler. She also loves to garden, read, and sing.

- Sharon has been called fun, curious, silly, present, and articulate. A colleague said, "Sharon has the presence of a wise woman wrapped in a spirit of lightness."

www.ingramcontent.com/pod-product-compliance
Lightning Source LLC
LaVergne TN
LVHW051514070426
835507LV00023B/3106